TERMEDIATE

T0036894

Best-Loved Hymns I
A Practical Anthology for Church and Home

Arranged by
Lyndell Leatherman

Production: Frank J. Hackinson
Production Coordinator: Satish Bhakta
Editors: Lyndell Leatherman and Edwin McLean
Cover: Keith Alexander
Engraving: Tempo Music Press, Inc.
Printer: Tempo Music Press, Inc.

T H E
F·J·H
M U S I C
COMPANY
I N C.
Frank J. Hackinson

ISBN-13: 978-1-56939-583-7

Contents

Foreword: A Singing Faith

From the early days of Christianity, hymns have been used successfully to reinforce and spread doctrine and faith. Scholars point out a number of hymn fragments in the New Testament.
For example, 1 Timothy 3:16 –

He appeared in a body,
Was vindicated by the Spirit,
Was seen by angels,
Was preached among the nations,
Was believed on in the world,
Was taken up into glory.

The metrical patterns made memorization of creeds easier, especially when associated with a melody.

The apostle Paul advised the Colossians to teach and help one another with psalms and hymns and spiritual songs *(Colossians 3:16)*. He was also aware of the evangelizing power of Christian song, due to experiences such as the one he shared with Silas in the Philippian jail *(Acts 16:25-31)*.

Centuries later, Martin Luther's strong belief in the importance of congregational song gave him a powerful boost in bringing about the Protestant Reformation. Likewise, the great revival that occurred in 18th-century England was propagated as much on the wings of Charles Wesley's hymns as on his brother John's preaching. Finally, no discussion of the spiritual awakening that spread like wildfire through America during the 19th century would be complete without considerable credit going to the widespread use of the popular gospel hymns.

Today, 21st-century Christians enjoy a heritage of hymnody that is a composite of all that has happened before. And today, just as in the first century of Christianity, hymns are still a marvelous means of communicating our faith. When we sing "Holy, Holy, Holy," we confess our faith in the Triune God. When we sing "The Church's One Foundation," we declare our belief concerning the Church of Jesus Christ. And when we sing "How Firm a Foundation," we affirm our utter dependence on the written Word of God.

While spoken creeds are valuable in reinforcing sets of beliefs shared by a congregation, confessions of faith set to music open the door for the added dimension of emotion–a component often lacking in the corporate recitation of creeds. The hymnal has been called the layman's theology textbook. Indeed, it does contain a vast wealth of theology, just waiting to be confirmed in the hearts of God's people and expressed outwardly through His wonderful gift of music.

Lyndell Leatherman

A Note About Performance Options

This volume is designed for maximum flexibility of use.
Please note:

1. Each arrangement may be played as a piano solo, for service use or personal enjoyment. Unless otherwise indicated, the small notes in the bass clef are for organ pedals, and thus are unneeded by (and awkward for) the pianist. Don't even think of playing them!

2. All but a few of the arrangements work equally well as organ solos. (The exceptions are flagged with a notice below the first system.) Except where indicated, play the lowest note of the bass clef on the pedals. Sometimes small notes are added for organ pedal use; in those passages, play all of the other bass clef notes on the manual.

3. The same arrangements that work for organ will work as organ-piano duets. Most church musicians will find this material instantly sightreadable—thus a practical source of short preludes, offertories, and postludes that don't require extensive rehearsal time.

4. The hymn texts are provided, making the volume a handy resource for solo or group singing, or personal edification.

5. Chord symbols are provided, along with a guitar chord chart on page 160. In light of the burgeoning praise and worship movement in the Church today, this should prove useful for guitarists and/or electric bass players. Remember that in the case of stacked chord symbols, the guitarist plays the "numerator" and the bassist plays the "denominator."

6. A fully-notated introduction is included in most cases, but where space didn't allow such, the intro is suggested with a bracket. If using the arrangement as an offertory or "traveling music," you may choose to omit the intro altogether.

7. Each arrangement contains an optional repeat back to the beginning of the stanza. This is primarily in case someone is singing along and desires to sing multiple stanzas, but it also allows for optional stretching of the length if using the arrangement as a prelude or offertory.

8. There are no organ registrations and very few dynamic markings included. Because the circumstances of performance vary so widely, it's assumed that the performer will use his or her best judgment on these matters—taking into consideration the nature of the hymn, the acoustical environment, the best registrations of the instrument at hand, and the context of the service in which the arrangement is being used.

A Note About the Compilation Process

Having been previously involved in the process of compiling and editing a denominational hymnal, I knew that there is a core group of hymns which are considered "non-negotiables" when it comes to producing new hymnals. These are the best of all that's happened before, the "cream of the crop," the psalms, hymns, and spiritual songs that have withstood the test of time and have become the standards by which all newcomers are measured.

When compiling this volume, I wanted to make sure that the core group I had in mind wasn't limited to one denomination or tradition. So I turned to my friend Rick Deasley at Tempo Publications of Leawood, Kansas, who has developed marvelous worship planning software known as *Service Designer®. Because it has an interactive database of thousands of hymns (and I use the word "hymns" in this context to include the genre of contemporary songs often referred to as "praise & worship" music), I asked for the privilege of tapping into his research. Checking 24 of the most influential hymnals published since 1970, he gave me a comprehensive list of hymns in order of their frequency of inclusion. The 75 selections in *Best-Loved Hymns I* were the ones most frequently included in this broad spectrum of hymnals–whether denominationally sponsored or independently produced. ("How Great Thou Art" was also included in the top 75 most used hymns, but is omitted here due to licensing complications.)

For those of us involved in worship planning and leadership, I would suggest that we need to make sure that our children, our youth, and our congregations are given ample opportunities to become familiar with this body of hymnody. Even if the regular fare of our local church is praise & worship music, let's find ways of resetting, revising, or revisiting these standards that connect us with the Church Universal-both past and present. Otherwise, these hymns could be one generation away from extinction, and that would be to the Church's detriment, in this editor's humble opinion.

Lyndell Leatherman

* For more information about Service Designer®,
  visit www.tempomusic.com

A Note About the Hymn Background Information

The hymn backgrounds in this collection are summaries of pertinent details gleaned from a variety of sources—12 books and a folder of magazine articles collected over the last quarter century. It was a labor of love to sift through the available information. In some cases, my sources showed minor discrepancies between dates or sequences of events, and I had to determine where the weight of evidence landed. If there is a hymnologist who can document errors in this volume, please contact me via the publisher and we will be happy to make corrections at the next reprinting.

As I researched the history of these hymns, a couple of general observations came to mind:

1. Often the most beautiful poetry and song comes out of brokenness or tragedy in a person's life. That suggests that while we may not feel like embracing hardships in our lives, we should seek to understand the lessons that we can extract from such experiences.

2. One can't help but notice the high percentage of standard English hymnody that was written by clergy. Ministers of today, have you ever thought of writing a hymn to summarize your sermon? To start, take an existing public domain tune that your congregation knows, and write a text to fit. You even have available resources that the ancients didn't have: a thesaurus and a rhyming dictionary–two important tools for poets. (You might even find that these are included in the word processing program on your computer.) If it is true that, as the saying goes, the hymnal is the layman's theology textbook, then it seems to follow that hymnwriting is too important to be left exclusively to amateur theologians!

Lyndell Leatherman

Index of Hymn Tunes

Index of Authors, Translators, and Composers

Index of Topics, Seasons, and Occasions

A Mighty Fortress Is Our God

In 1517 the audacious monk, Martin Luther, nailed a document to the door of the Wittenberg Castle Church–outlining 95 objections to the Roman Church's practice of selling indulgences. In the storm that followed, he was excommunicated, branded a heretic, and forced into exile. Four years later, when it was relatively safe to do so, he returned to Wittenberg, and there he plunged into a life of constant activity: preaching, teaching, writing, and organizing a reform movement. As he was molding the evangelical church in Germany, Luther felt the need for a new kind of service music to take the place of Latin chants. He set about to produce "German psalms for the people–spiritual songs, that is, whereby the Word of God may be kept alive in them by singing." At first he tried to persuade some of his colleagues to supply these needed hymns. When there was only a meager response, he undertook the task himself, publishing his first hymnbook in 1524. In all, Luther is thought to have written 37 hymns, only a few of which are still known today. His best-known effort, "A Mighty Fortress Is Our God," spread like a forest fire all over Germany. It was based on Ps. 34: "God is our refuge and strength, a very present help in trouble," and people took it to heart at first hearing. The hymn's popularity has continued to spread until today, by last count, it has been translated into 184 languages worldwide. The original tune was similar in contour to the tune we use today, but faster and syncopated (see illustration–the hymn as found in the *Klugschen* songbook, published in 1533).

Martin Luther, 1529
Tr. by Frederick H. Hedge, 1852

EIN' FESTE BURG
Martin Luther, 1529

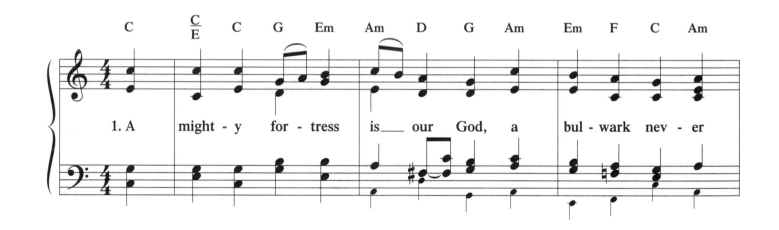

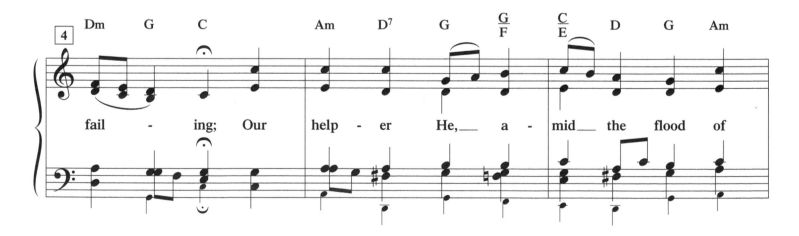

2. Did we in our own strength confide,
   Our striving would be losing;
   Were not the right Man on our side,
   The Man of God's own choosing.
   Dost ask who that may be?
   Christ Jesus, it is He,
   Lord Sabaoth His name,
   From age to age the same,
   And He must win the battle.

3. And though this world, with devils filled,
   Should threaten to undo us,
   We will not fear, for God hath willed
   His truth to triumph through us.
   The prince of darkness grim,
   We tremble not for him.
   His rage we can endure,
   For, lo, his doom is sure;
   One little word shall fell him.

4. That Word above all earthly pow'rs,
   No thanks to them, abideth;
   The spirit and the gift are ours
   Through Him who with us sideth.
   Let goods and kindred go,
   This mortal life also.
   The body they may kill;
   God's truth abideth still.
   His kingdom is forever.

Abide with Me

Henry Francis Lyte was born in Kelso, Ireland in 1793. When Henry was quite young, his father died, necessitating a family move to Dublin. There he succeeded in graduating from college, earning several prizes in poetry along the way. Though he had initially hoped to become a physician, he decided while in college to enter the ministry. Ordained by the Church of England at age 22, he applied himself diligently to the work of the pastorate for eight years. During this time he began to show symptoms of tuberculosis. At that time in history, this disease baffled the medical profession, but Lyte was led to believe that the salt air of a coastal town would be helpful in his battle against the dreaded lung ailment. So he accepted an assignment to the parish at Brixham-on-Sea, England, populated mainly by sailors and fisherfolk. For nearly a quarter of a century he labored here, though he was forced to periodically winter in warmer climates. In the early autumn of 1847, he observed that the swallows were flying southward once again, inviting him to accompany them. "But alas," he wrote, "while I am talking of flying, I am just able to crawl." His doctors had told him that he could no longer work, but must permanently move to the drier, warmer environment of Italy to have any chance of survival. So on Sept. 4, the farewell Sunday came. Though admonished by friends and family not to attempt to preach in his exhausted condition, he insisted on doing so. He took as his text Luke 24:29 (KJV), where Jesus met the two disciples on the road to Emmaus and at their request–"Abide with us, for it is toward evening, and the day is far spent"–ate dinner with them. The service had a real poignancy for his flock, who seemed to have a premonition that this might be the last time they would hear their beloved shepherd speak. That afternoon, with the prayer of the disciples lingering in his mind, along with the sense of his own mortality looming heavy on the horizon, Lyte retired to his room where he wrote the eight-stanza text "Abide with Me" in the space of about an hour. He handed the manuscript to his adopted daugher, who placed it in a trunk for safekeeping. That week, after many tearful goodbyes, he departed for Italy. However, his rapidly declining health made it impossible to go any farther than Nice, France, and it was there that he died on Nov. 20, 1847, at the age of 54. In 1861, a group of ministers within the Church of England published a collection, *Hymns Ancient and Modern*, which, with its subsequent editions, was to become the most widely used hymnal of all time in the English-speaking world. Lyte's "swan song" had recently come to the attention of its music editor, William H. Monk, director of the choir of King's College, London. Replacing Lyte's original melody with one of his own, Monk included "Abide with Me" in this monumental hymnal, and thus a timeless classic was introduced to the world.

It should also be noted that Lyte had earlier in his lifetime written such standards as "Jesus, I My Cross Have Taken" and "Praise, My Soul, the King of Heaven."

EVENTIDE
William H. Monk, 1861

Henry F. Lyte, 1847

(this arrangement not recommended for use with organ)

*Quoting Ludwig van Beethoven's "Adagio Cantabile" from *Pathétique Sonata, Op. 13*.

2. Swift to its close ebbs out life's little day;
   Earth's joys grow dim, its glories pass away.
   Change and decay in all around I see;
   O Thou who changest not, abide with me!

3. I need Thy presence ev'ry passing hour;
   What but Thy grace can foil the tempter's power?
   Who like Thyself my guide and stay can be?
   I triumph still, if Thou abide with me!

4. I fear no foe, with Thee at hand to bless;
   Ills have no weight, and tears no bitterness.
   Where is death's sting? Where, grave, thy victory?
   I triumph still if Thou abide with me!

5. Hold Thou Thy cross before my closing eyes;
   Shine through the gloom and point me to the skies.
   Heav'n's morning breaks, and earth's vain shadows flee;
   In life, in death, O Lord, abide with me.

FJH2023

All Creatures of Our God and King

Francis of Assisi was born into a wealthy Italian family in 1182. As a devout young man, he renounced his life of ease and became a traveling evangelist–working with and preaching to the peasants who scratched out their livelihoods in the countrysides. For 14 years he toured the countries surrounding the Mediterranean, proclaiming a dual message of love for Christ and love for one's fellow man. Not only did Francis minister to the large crowds of people who met him everywhere he went, but legend says that he possessed a special gift for communicating with animals. Indeed, because of his great love for and affinity with all of God's creatures, he became known as the patron saint of animals. During the hot summer of 1225, as Francis lay in his straw hut very ill and losing his sight, he penned in Italian the poem which was 700 years later translated "All Creatures of Our God and King." The next year, 1226, he died at the age of 44.

The melody LASST UNS ERFREUEN is of unknown origin, first appearing in the Roman Catholic hymnal *Geistlische Kirchengesang,* published in 1623. When the so-called high church wing of the the Church of England published *The English Hymnal* in 1906, their music editor–the brilliant composer, Ralph Vaughan Williams (1872-1958)–included his new harmonization of the tune as a setting for the hymn text, "Ye Watchers and Ye Holy Ones." In 1925, when William H. Draper translated Francis' ancient poem into English, he crafted it to fit the anonymous German hymntune that had so recently been revitalized by Vaughan Williams' definitive arrangement.

Francis of Assisi, 1225
Tr. by William H. Draper, 1925

LASST UNS ERFREUEN
Anonymous German Hymntune
Harm. by Ralph Vaughan Williams, 1906

Arrangement produced by permission of Oxford University Press. All Rights Reserved.

2. Thou rushing wind that are so strong,
   Ye clouds that sail in heav'n along,
   O praise Him! Alleluia!
   Thou rising morn, in praise rejoice;
   Ye lights of evening, find a voice!
   O praise Him! O praise Him!
   Alleluia! Alleluia! Alleluia!

3. Thou flowing water, pure and clear,
   Make music for thy Lord to hear.
   Alleluia! Alleluia!
   Thou fire so masterful and bright,
   Thou givest man both warmth and light!
   O praise Him! O praise Him!
   Alleluia! Alleluia! Alleluia!

4. Dear mother earth, who day by day
   Unfoldest blessings on our way,
   O praise Him! Alleluia!
   The flowers and fruits that in thee grow,
   Let them His glory also show!
   O praise Him! O praise Him!
   Alleluia! Alleluia! Alleluia!

5. And all ye men of tender heart,
   Forgiving others, take your part.
   O sing ye! Alleluia!
   Ye who long pain and sorrow bear,
   Praise God and on Him cast your care!
   O praise Him! O praise Him!
   Alleluia! Alleluia! Alleluia!

6. Let all things their Creator bless,
   And worship Him in humbleness.
   O praise Him! Alleluia!
   Praise, praise the Father, praise the Son,
   And praise the Spirit, Three in One!
   O praise Him! O praise Him!
   Alleluia! Alleluia! Alleluia!

All Glory, Laud, and Honor

Theodulph was born in Italy around 760 A.D. As a young man he entered into monastic life, where his great piety coupled with unusual intelligence soon advanced him to the position of abbot. His obvious skill as a mediator caught the attention of Charlemagne, who was in Italy at the time. Upon returning to France, the conqueror took Theodulph with him and installed him as the Bishop of Orleans. This appointment of a foreigner stirred up envy among lesser men. When Charlemagne's son–Louis the Pious–assumed the reign shortly thereafter, these men conspired against Theodulph and had him imprisoned in Angers, where he languished for three years. But his confinement was not totally in vain, for during this time he authored a poetic rendering of the Triumphal Entry–a Latin hymn of 39 stanzas, entitled "Gloria, Laus et Honor." According to legend, on Palm Sunday of 820, King Louis and his retinue were processing through the streets of Angers on their way to church. As they paused near the prison tower, they heard the newly-composed hymn being chanted by a strong, mellifluous voice. Upon inquiry, the emporer learned that the mystery vocalist was none other than the great pastor and bishop who had been jailed on suspicion of treachery against the crown. As the story goes, the monarch's heart was moved to compassion, and in that same hour he had Theodulph pardoned, released from prison, and reinstalled in his church with full royal favor. Unfortunately, the pastor-poet died the next year, in 821. Some time later, he was canonized a saint. His greatest legacy, the most beloved Palm Sunday hymn of all time, shows no hint of the dark, dank environment in which it was written. Like the Apostle Paul, John Bunyan, Dietrich Bonhoffer, and so many others who have inspired the world with their prison writings, Theodulph was a man whose soul could not be shackled.

John Mason Neale (1818-1866) was a minister in the Church of England. Caught up in the Oxford Movement, he became interested in the original languages–specifically, Greek, and Latin–that had cradled the early liturgies of the Church. He became a renowned translator of ancient hymns–among them, "Of the Father's Love Begotten," "O Come, O Come, Emmanuel," "Good Christian Men, Rejoice," and "All Glory, Laud, and Honor."

Theodulph of Orleans, ca. 820
Tr. by John M. Neale, 1854

ST. THEODULPH
Melchior Teschner, 1615

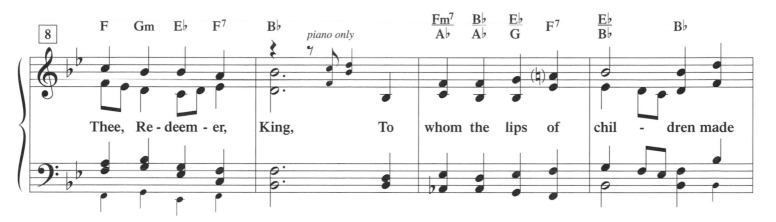

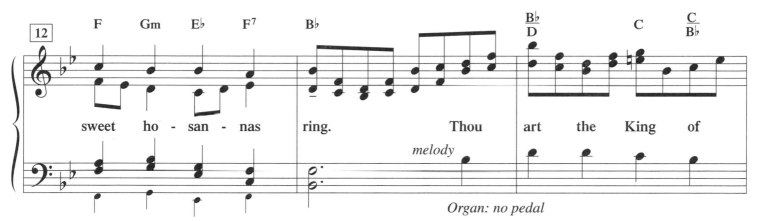

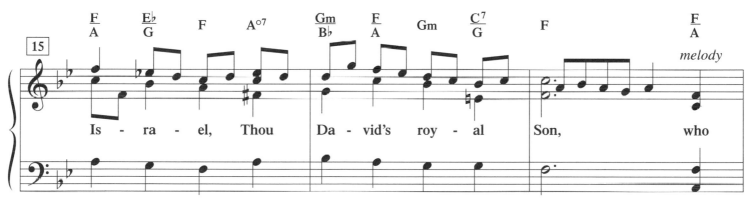

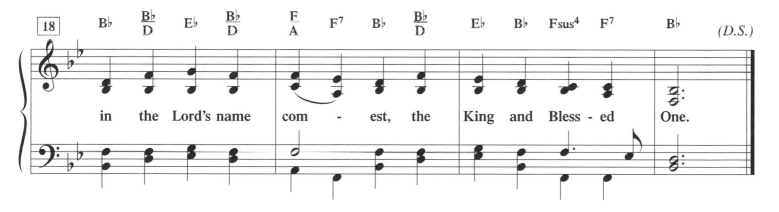

2. The company of angels
   Are praising Thee on high,
   And mortal men and all things
   Created make reply.
   The people of the Hebrews
   With palms before Thee went;
   Our praise and prayer and anthems
   Before Thee we present.

3. To Thee, before Thy passion,
   They sang their hymns of praise–
   To Thee, now high exalted,
   Our melody we raise.
   Thou didst accept their praises;
   Accept the praise we bring,
   Who in all good delightest,
   Thou good and gracious King.

All Hail the Power of Jesus' Name

The hymn text known today as "All Hail the Power of Jesus' Name" was written in England in 1779 by Edward Perronet (1726-1792), son of a clergyman in the Church of England. Perronet, himself an Anglican minister, was sympathetic to the cause of John and Charles Wesley, the founders of Methodism, even to the point of being roughed up by a mob on one occasion as he traveled with the itinerant preachers. His poem of eight stanzas, originally entitled "The Lord Is King," first appeared anonymously in 1780 in the *Gospel Magazine,* a periodical edited by Augustus Toplady (most famous as the author of "Rock of Ages"). In 1787, John Rippon included the poem in his *Baptist Hymnal,* at which time he wrote and added the summary stanza that begins, "Oh, that with yonder sacred throng..." Perronet wrote three volumes of sacred poems in his lifetime, but all are forgotten except for this one. He spent his later life in relative obscurity, pastoring a small nonconformist chapel.

The text has been strongly associated with three different tunes. MILES LANE has been used primarily in England, and the very melismatic DIADEM was more popular in the hymn's earlier days. CORONATION, composed in 1792 by Oliver Holden (1765-1844), of Charlestown, Massachusetts, has become the tune of choice in most of the hymnals produced in the United States during the last century. Holden had many careers during his lifetime. He began as a carpenter, then dabbled in real estate, then owned a music store, then became an author, a publisher, a representative in Congress, and finally, a lay preacher.

Edward Perronet, 1779
Alt. by John Rippon, 1787

CORONATION
Oliver Holden, 1792

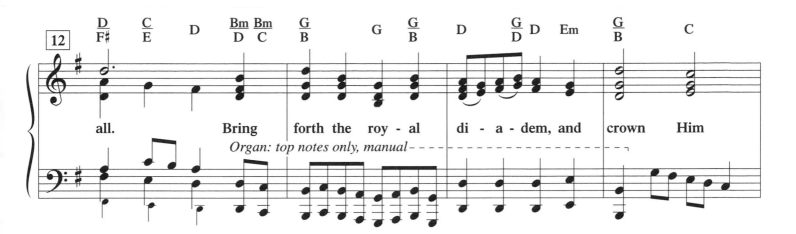

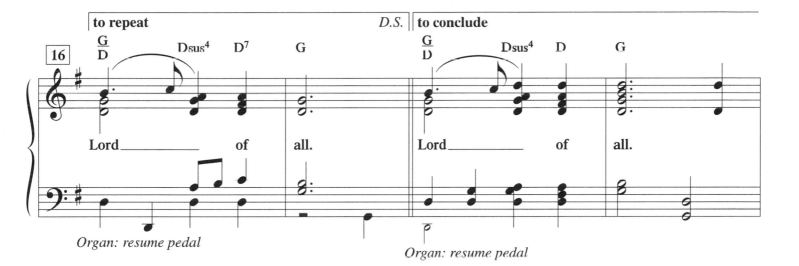

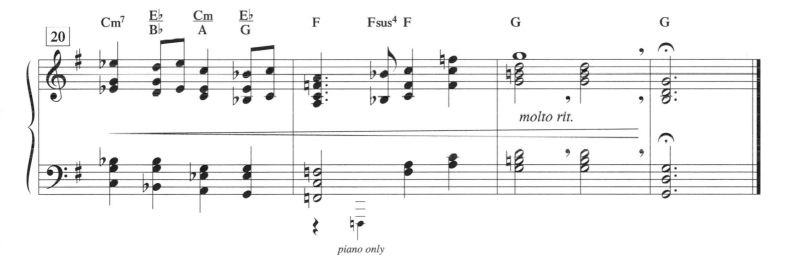

2. Ye chosen seed of Israel's race,
   Ye ransomed from the fall,
   Hail Him who saves you by His grace,
   And crown Him Lord of all.
   Hail Him who saves you by His grace,
   And crown Him Lord of all.

3. Let ev'ry kindred, ev'ry tribe
   On this terrestrial ball
   To Him all majesty ascribe,
   And crown Him Lord of all.
   To Him all majesty ascribe,
   And crown Him Lord of all.

4. Oh, that with yonder sacred throng
   We at His feet may fall!
   We'll join the everlasting song
   And crown Him Lord of all.
   We'll join the everlasting song
   And crown Him Lord of all.

FJH2023

Amazing Grace

John Newton was born in London in 1725. His mother was a quiet, devout woman and his father was an austere shipmaster who was rarely home. As a young lad, John was taught the basics of the Christian faith at the knee of his mother, whom he adored. But when he was seven she died from tuberculosis, and John's idyllic world came crashing in, leading to a tumultuous and rebellious childhood. After a couple of apprenticeships as a sailor, during which time John strayed from the faith, he was impressed into the British navy at the age of 20. Finding the conditions deplorable, he deserted. Arrested two days later, he was flogged and then transferred to duty on a slave ship. At this point he was a rabid atheist, and "exceedingly vile," as he later confessed. For two years his life spiraled downward, finally reaching rock bottom as he himself became the servant of an abusive slave trader in Sierra Leone. His father, knowing that he was involved in this nefarious business but having lost track of his whereabouts, put out the request to ship owners to find him and bring him home. Providentially, the captain of the slave ship Greyhound crossed paths with him and allowed him to board the vessel for the long journey back to England by way of Brazil. Out of sheer boredom, Newton picked up Thomas á Kempis' *The Imitation of Christ*. Though it disturbed him greatly, wicked as he was, it nevertheless planted seeds in his mind. Later that same voyage, a violent storm nearly sank the ship, bringing Newton to his knees. Surviving the storm, he continued in the slave trade for another four years. However, the trauma of that journey had set events in motion that would eventually transform Newton into a minister of the Gospel, a social reformer, and a hymn writer. Throughout his long life, he teamed up with men like William Wilberforce and John Wesley to crusade against slavery. Finally, in March of 1807, Parliament passed Wilberforce's bill abolishing the British slave trade. Later that same year, the 82-yr-old Newton died. His last words: "I am a great sinner...and Christ is a great Savior."

St. 1-4: John Newton, 1779
St. 5: Anonymous, date unknown

AMAZING GRACE
Anonymous
From *Virginia Harmony*, 1831

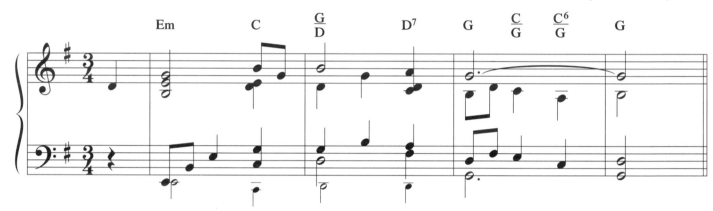

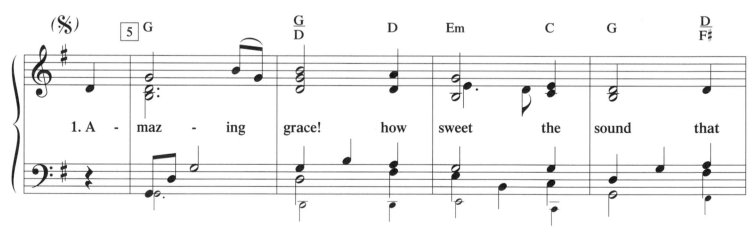

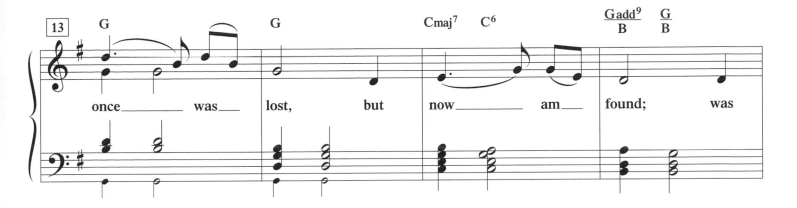

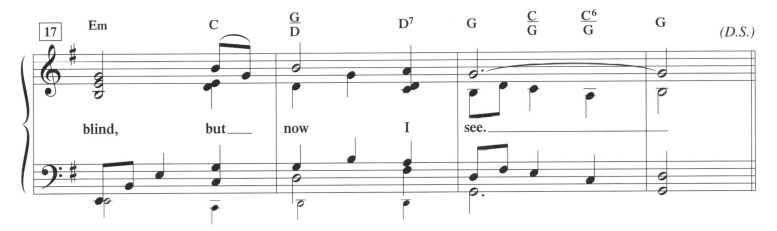

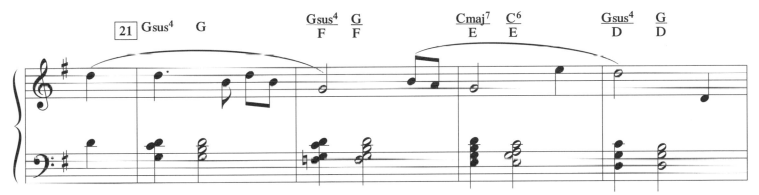

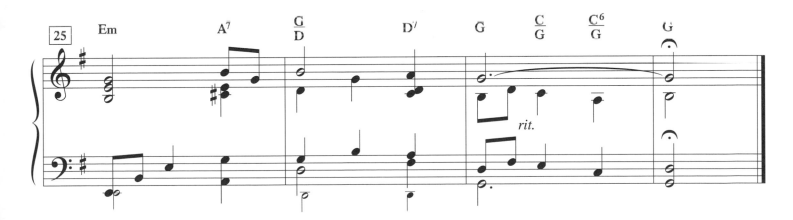

2. 'Twas grace that taught my heart to fear,
And grace my fears relieved.
How precious did that grace appear
The hour I first believed.

4. Through many dangers, toils, and snares
I have already come.
'Tis grace hath brought me safe thus far,
And grace will lead me home.

3. The Lord has promised good to me;
His Word my hope secures.
He will my shield and portion be
As long as life endures.

5. When we've been there ten thousand years
Bright, shining as the sun,
We've no less days to sing God's praise
Than when we'd first begun.

FJH2023

Angels from the Realms of Glory

When ranking the contributions of those who have shaped English hymnody, a good case could be made for placing James Montgomery's immediately after those of Charles Wesley and Isaac Watts. During the course of his long life (1771-1854), he wrote some 400 hymns, including "Prayer Is the Soul's Sincere Desire," "Go to Dark Gethsemane," "In the Hour of Trial," "According to Thy Gracious Word," and "Angels from the Realms of Glory." Born in Scotland where his father was a minister, he was enrolled in a Moravian seminary in Yorkshire, England. Shortly thereafter, his parents were sent to the West Indies as missionaries. There they both contracted tropical diseases and died, making it impossible for James to continue his schooling. After two years of unsuccessful attempts to find a publisher for his poems, the 21-yr-old landed a job working with a radical newspaper publisher, Robert Gales. When Gales left for America to avoid prosecution, Montgomery, then 23, took over publication of the paper, changing its name from the *Sheffield Register* to the *Sheffield Iris*. Continuing the paper's tradition of political incorrectness, Montgomery spent two stints in prison during his first two years of editorship. From this experience came a book of poems in 1797, entitled appropriately, "Prison Amusements." Its popularity, along with that of the *Iris*, vindicated Montgomery, and his strong Christian faith–both in adversity and prosperity–eventually won the hearts and minds of the authorities. In later years, the British government even awarded him a sizeable pension in recognition of his achievements, and perhaps as a way of apologizing for his shoddy treatment as a young newspaper man. "Angels from the Realms of Glory" first appeared in the Christmas Eve 1816 edition of the *Iris*, and was republished in the 1825 hymnbook, *The Christian Psalmist.*

REGENT SQUARE
Henry T. Smart, 1867

James Montgomery, 1816

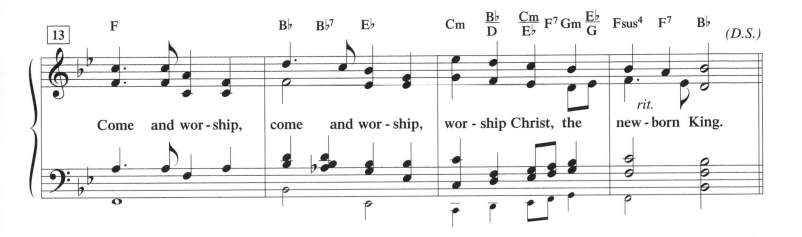

Come and wor-ship, come and wor-ship, wor-ship Christ, the new-born King.

Slightly broader

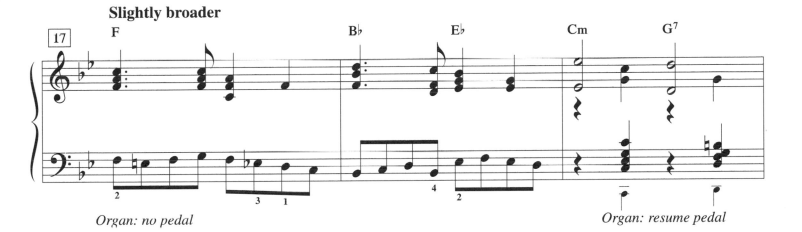

Organ: no pedal

Organ: resume pedal

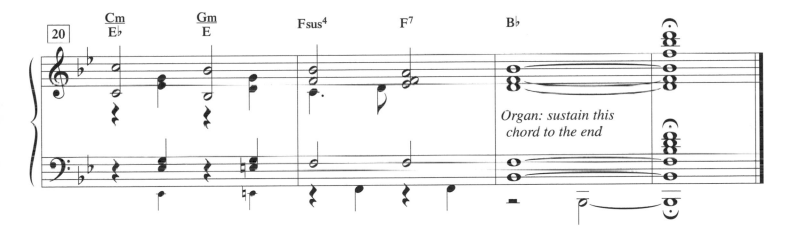

Organ: sustain this chord to the end

2. Shepherds, in the field abiding,
   Watching o'er your flocks by night,
   God with man is now residing;
   Yonder shines the Infant Light.
   Come and worship, come and worship,
   Worship Christ, the newborn King.

3. Sages, leave your contemplations;
   Brighter visions beam afar.
   Seek the great desire of nations;
   Ye have seen His natal star.
   Come and worship, come and worship,
   Worship Christ, the newborn King.

4. Saints before the altar bending,
   Watching long in hope and fear,
   Suddenly the Lord descending,
   In His temple shall appear.
   Come and worship, come and worship,
   Worship Christ, the newborn King.

Angels We Have Heard on High

Many years ago on Christmas Eve, as legend goes, shepherds in the south of France called to one another from neighboring peaks, singing the words used by the angel choir the night Christ was born: "gloria in excelsis Deo" (glory to God in the highest). The text and tune they used–the refrain of today's version of "Angels We Have Heard on High"–was based on a medieval Latin chorale. In 1855, an anonymous hymnal editor set the traditional French poem "Les Anges dans nos Campagnes" to a folk tune which was popular at the time, adding the melismatic refrain. Seven years later, the carol was first translated into English, appearing in an 1862 hymnbook, *Crown of Jesus Music*.

Traditional French Carol

GLORIA
Traditional French Melody

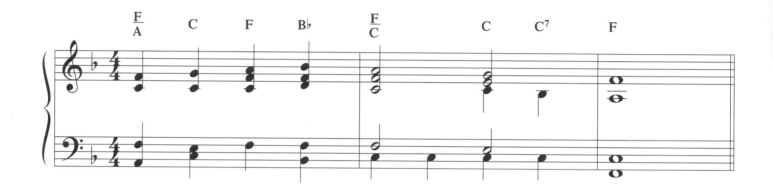

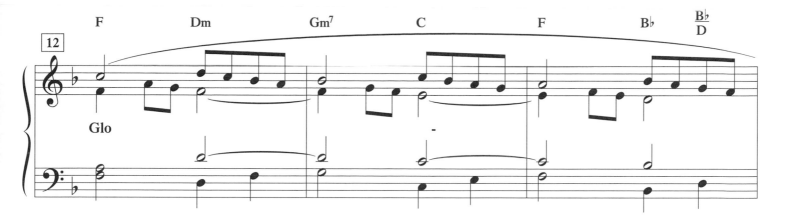

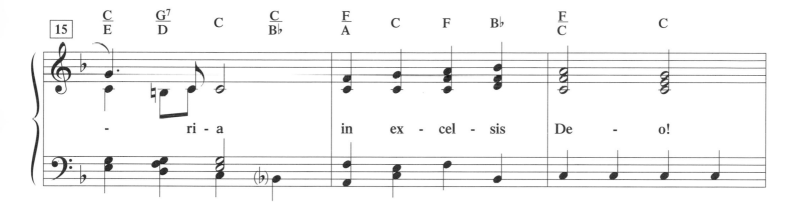

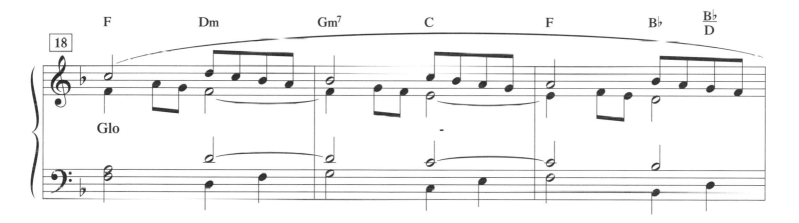

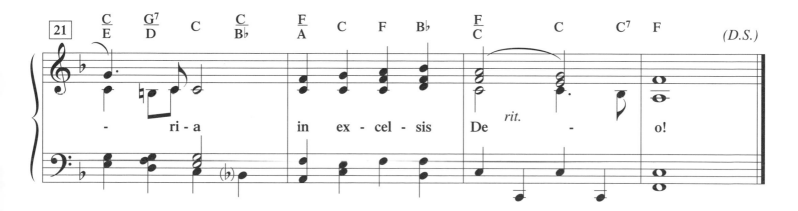

2. Shepherds, why this jubilee?
   Why your joyous strains prolong?
   What the gladsome tidings be
   Which inspire your heav'nly song?
   Gloria in excelsis Deo!
   Gloria in excelsis Deo!

3. Come to Bethlehem and see
   Him whose birth the angels sing;
   Come, adore on bended knee
   Christ the Lord, the newborn King.
   Gloria in excelsis Deo!
   Gloria in excelsis Deo!

Away in a Manger

The first two stanzas of "Away in a Manger" first appeared, anonymously, in 1885–in a collection entitled *Little Children's Book: For School and Families,* issued by the Evangelical Lutheran Church of North America. The tune used there, attributed to one J.F. Clark, never caught on. Two years later, in 1887, James R. Murray edited a kindergarden songbook, *Dainty Songs for Lads and Lasses,* for the John Church Company in Cincinnati. He included the anonymous Christmas text, setting it to a melody of his own–the one most commonly used today. In this collection he called the song "Luther's Cradle Song" and added the footnote: "Composed by Martin Luther for his children, and still sung by German mothers to their little ones." However, subsequent research revealed that the people in Germany were unaware of the song until it arrived from America sometime later. As is often the case, Murray had perpetuated a legend that had come to his attention without researching its credibility. In 1892, the famous American hymnwriter and editor, Charles H. Gabriel, published a collection, *Gabriel's Vineyard Songs,* in which he included the hymn with Murray's tune and a third stanza by one John Thomas McFarland. Sometime after World War I, the song appeared in a new volume, *Words and Song,* crediting the song to a Carl Mueller. But no one seems to know who Mueller was, and that credit is no longer given.

St. 1-2: Anonymous, 1885
St. 3: John Thomas McFarland, 1892

AWAY IN A MANGER
James R. Murray, 1887

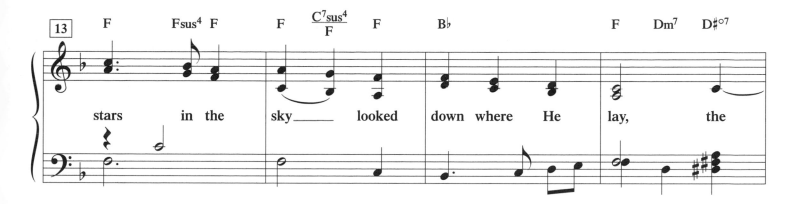

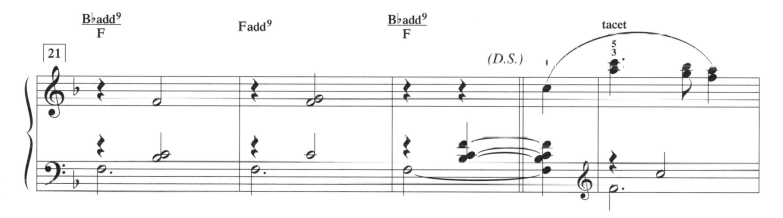

2. The cattle are lowing; the Baby awakes,
But little Lord Jesus–no crying he makes.
I love Thee, Lord Jesus; look down from the sky
And stay by my cradle till morning is nigh.

3. Be near me, Lord Jesus; I ask Thee to stay
Close by me forever, and love me, I pray.
Bless all the dear children in Thy tender care,
And fit us for heaven, to live with Thee there.

Be Thou My Vision

Very little is known about the origins of this ancient hymn text, other than the fact that it came from Ireland sometime around the 8th century. In 1905, it was translated into English prose by the Irishwoman Mary Byrne (1880-1931). Seven years later, her compatriot–Eleanor Hull (1860-1935)–turned the prose back into poetry, or versified it, if you will. Their collaboration included the following as stanza three, a verse rarely seen in hymnals today:

Be Thou my breastplate, my sword for the fight;
Thou my whole armor and Thou my true might;
Thou my soul's shelter, Thou my strong tower.
Raise Thou me heav'nward, great Power of my power.

Traditional Irish Hymn, ca. 8th century
Tr. by Mary E. Byrne, 1905

SLANE
Traditional Irish Melody

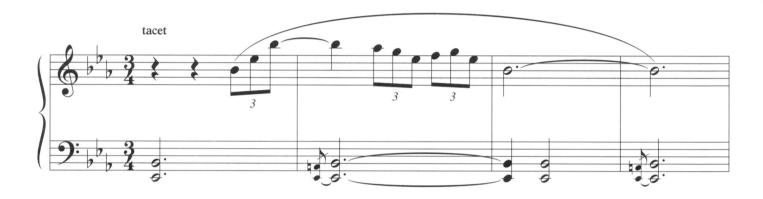

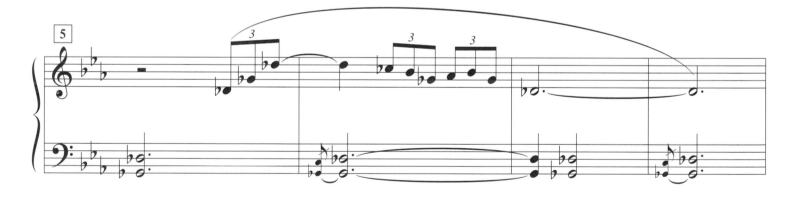

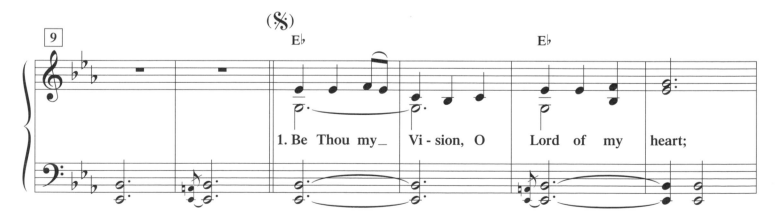

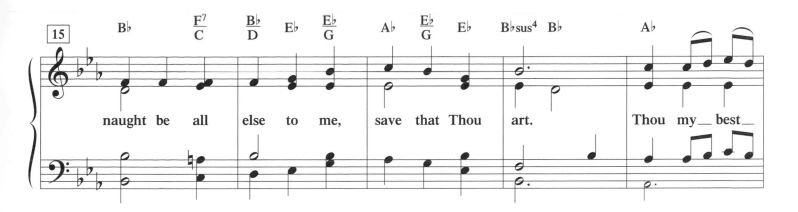

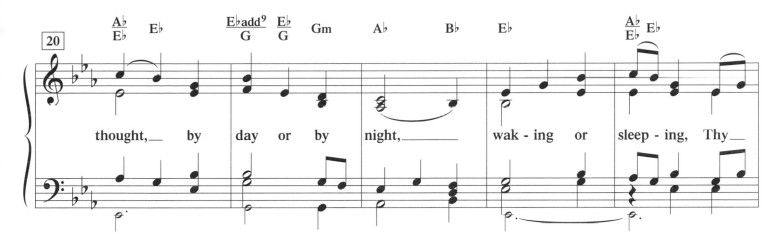

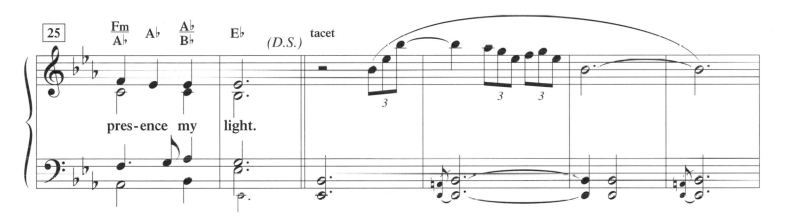

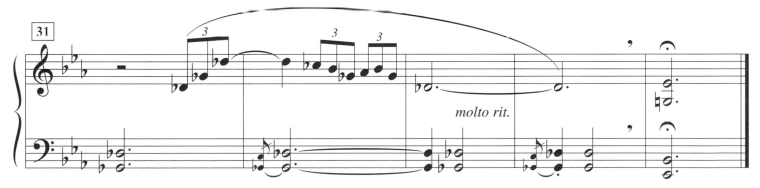

2. Be Thou my Wisdom, and Thou my true Word;
   I ever with Thee and Thou with me, Lord;
   Thou my great Father, I Thy true son;
   Thou in me dwelling, and I with Thee one.

3. Riches I heed not, nor man's empty praise,
   Thou mine inheritance, now and always;
   Thou and Thou only, first in my heart,
   High King of Heaven, my Treasure Thou art.

4. High King of Heaven, my victory won,
   May I reach heaven's joys, Bright Heaven's Sun!
   Heart of my own heart, whatever befall,
   Still be my Vision, O Ruler of all.

Beneath the Cross of Jesus

The text, "Beneath the Cross of Jesus," was written by Elizabeth C. Clephane, a Scottish hymnwriter. Born in 1830, Elizabeth was very quiet and reserved as a child, usually absorbed in her books. She lost both parents while quite young. In her adult life she was noted for her untiring work among the poor and outcast of Edinburgh, earning the nickname "Sunbeam." This text, along with that of the well-loved "The Ninety and Nine," was written in 1868 as Elizabeth lay terminally ill. After her death in 1869, both poems appeared posthumously in an article entitled "Breathings on the Border," which appeared in a periodical known as *The Family Treasury*. Part of the editor's introduction read as follows:

"...Written on the very edge of this life, with the better land fully in view,
they seem to us like footsteps on the sands of time, where the sands touch the ocean of eternity."

Sadly, Miss Clephane died at the age of 39 without ever hearing her immortal texts set to music.

The tune which has been inextricably linked with this ode to the cross is appropriately named ST. CHRISTOPHER, with the etymological meaning of "Christopher" being "bearer of Christ." Written in 1881, its composer, Frederick C. Maker (1844-1927), was an English composer of anthems.

Elizabeth C. Clephane, 1868

ST. CRISTOPHER
Frederick C. Maker, 1881

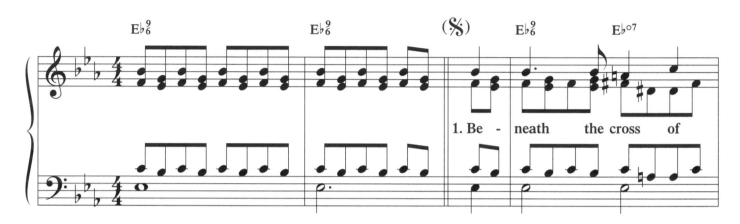

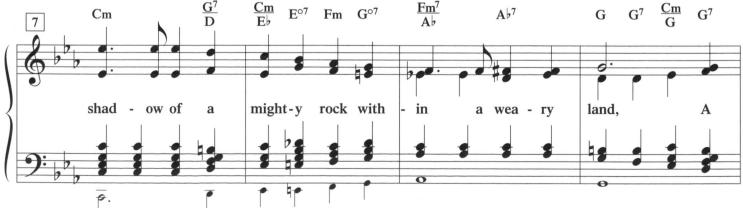

31

2. There lies beneath its shadow,
   But on the farther side,
   The darkness of an awful grave
   That gapes both deep and wide;
   And there between us stands the cross,
   Two arms outstretched to save,
   Like a watchman set to guard the way
   From that eternal grave.

3. Upon the cross of Jesus
   Mine eyes at times can see
   The very dying form of One
   Who suffered there for me.
   And from my smitten heart, with tears,
   These wonders I confess:
   The wonder of His glorious love,
   And my unworthiness.

4. I take, O cross, thy shadow
   For my abiding place.
   I ask no other sunshine than
   The sunshine of His face;
   Content to let the world go by,
   To know no gain nor loss,
   My sinful self—my only shame,
   My glory—all the cross.

Blessed Assurance

Phoebe Palmer Knapp (1839-1908) was born in New York City and was the daughter of the Methodist evangelist, Walter C. Palmer. She married Joseph Fairfield Knapp, a founder of the Metropolitan Life Insurance Company. She wrote more than 500 hymns and was widely respected as a hymn tune composer during her lifetime. On one occasion she visited her blind poetess friend, Fanny Crosby (1820-1915), and played this happy, lilting melody which she had recently composed. "What does the tune say?" she asked her host. Crosby didn't hesitate with her reply: "It says, 'Blessed assurance, Jesus is mine!'" Seizing the moment, she went on to write the remaining text on the spot. This amazing lady, rendered sightless while a baby because of a physician's error, is thought to have written 8,000 hymn texts in her lifetime, many of which are still found in hymnals today. Rather than considering her handicap an affliction, she deemed it a blessing, saying, "When I get to heaven, the first face that shall ever gladden my sight will be that of my Savior."

ASSURANCE
Phoebe Palmer Knapp, 1873

Fanny J. Crosby, 1873

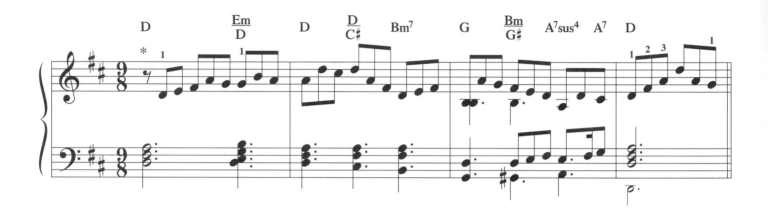

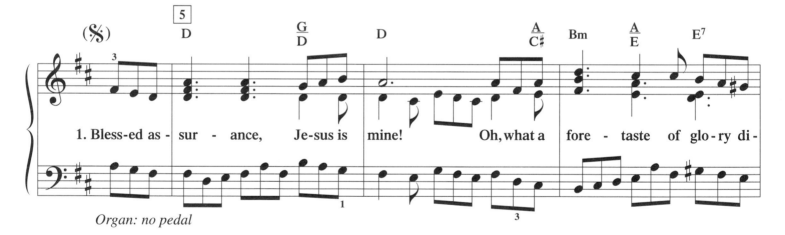

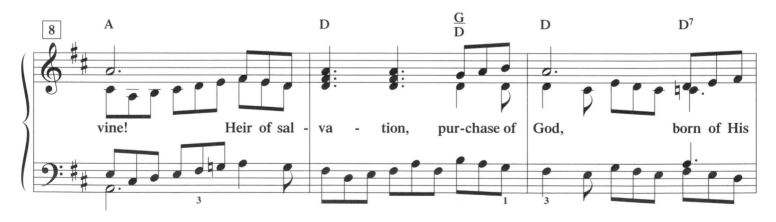

*Quoting J.S. Bach's "Jesu, Joy of Man's Desiring."

FJH2023

Organ: resume pedal

to repeat *D.S.*

to conclude

2. Perfect submission, perfect delight!
   Visions of rapture now burst on my sight!
   Angels descending bring from above
   Echoes of mercy, whispers of love.

   This is my story...

3. Perfect submission, all is at rest.
   I in my Savior am happy and blest;
   Watching and waiting, looking above,
   Filled with His goodness, lost in His love.

   This is my story...

FJH2023

Blest Be the Tie That Binds

John Fawcett (1740-1817) was the pastor of a modest Baptist congregation at Wainsgate, Yorkshire, England. Orphaned at the age of 12, Fawcett had worked long hours each day in a factory. Always highly motivated, he learned to read by candlelight, and applied himself to his studies. Ordained in 1765 at the age of 25, he and his family had accepted the call to this small church for the equivalent of one hundred dollars a year–partly paid with wool and potatoes. It had been a joyful time. In the seven years since his arrival, attendance had increased to the point that a gallery had to be built in the meetinghouse. The simple, unlettered members of the congregation–mostly shepherds and farmers–were loved by the pastor and his family, and the affection was reciprocal. Yet due to the general poverty in his parish, Fawcett's financial situation was always perilous. As his children grew older, their needs became more and more critical. Then one day, out of the blue, a wonderful opportunity came his way: he was invited to pastor London's great Carter Lane Church. The substantial stipend they offered would mean an end to the family's monetary struggles. Fawcett accepted the call, and on the appointed day gave his farewell sermon. The next day the moving wagons were loaded up as the entire congregation gathered to say goodbye. But their collective outpouring of grief proved to be too much for the parsonage family to bear, and in an instant they changed their minds and instructed that the wagons were to be unloaded–they were staying put. That week, as he reflected on the unusual turn of events, Fawcett wrote "Blest Be the Tie That Binds," and it was sung the following Sunday. The original text included two additional stanzas usually absent from hymnals today:

One glorious hope revives
Our courage by the way:
While each in expectation lives,
And longs to see the day.

When from all toil and pain
And sin we shall be free,
And perfect love and friendship reigns
Through all eternity.

Fawcett remained in Wainsgate 45 more years–to the end of his life. The richness of friendship and reputation more than compensated for the loss of pecuniary reward. He became one of Britain's most respected scholars and preachers. He wrote books, founded a school for young preachers, and published a volume of hymns–including another one still used today, "Lord, Dismiss Us with Thy Blessing." He even declined an offer from the monarch of that time–King George III–preferring to live among the rustic people he loved. He had learned the lesson that many miss: he who has good friends in this life is rich indeed.

DENNIS
John Fawcett, 1772

Johann G. Nägeli, 1828

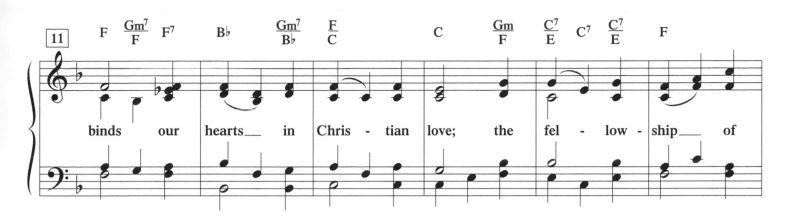

binds our hearts___ in Chris-tian love; the fel-low-ship___ of

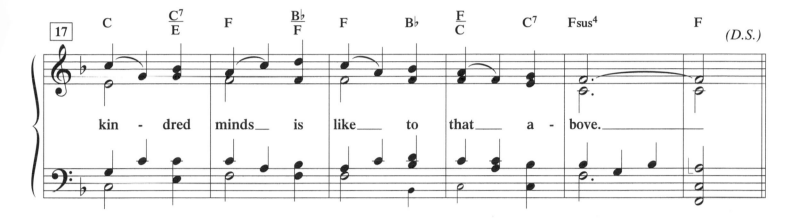

kin-dred minds___ is like___ to that___ a-bove.___

2. Before our Father's throne
   We pour our ardent prayers;
   Our fears, our hopes,
   our aims are one,
   Our comforts and our cares.

3. We share our mutual woes,
   Our mutual burdens bear;
   And often for each other flows
   The sympathizing tear.

4. When we asunder part,
   It gives us inward pain;
   But we shall soon be joined in heart,
   And hope to meet again.

FJH2023

Break Thou the Bread of Life

Mary Artimisia Lathbury (1841-1913) was born in Manchester, New York, the daughter of a Methodist minister. When she was quite young, her artistic and literary talents became readily apparent as she wrote several children's story books, illustrating them herself. These, along with her many poems and illustrations in magazines, made her quite well known in her day. In 1874, John Vincent, then secretary of the Methodist Sunday School Union, invited her to be his assistant. The Chautauqua movement–with its new facility built on the beautiful lake from which it took its name–had just been launched the previous year, and Dr. Vincent was named its leader. Knowing of Lathbury's writing skills, he commissioned several hymns. When Chautauqua's Literary and Scientific Circle was inaugurated, she was called on to write "a study song for members to sing at their gatherings over the country." A short time later, while meditating on the shore of the lake, she was inspired by the story of Christ's feeding of the multitude by the Sea of Galilee, as recorded in Mark 14. Making the application that Christ feeds us spiritual food today–through His Word, through His Spirit, and through the sacrament of holy communion–she crafted the poem "Break Thou the Bread of Life." Instantly popular at the Chautauqua meetings, it also became a favorite of the great London preacher, G. Campbell Morgan, who used it regularly before his midweek sermon.

Three years later, in 1880, Lathbury wrote the other hymn for which she is remembered today–"Day Is Dying in the West"–as the official vesper hymn for Chautauqua.

St. 1-3, 6: Mary A. Lathbury, 1877
St. 4-5: Alexander Groves, 1913

BREAD OF LIFE
William F. Sherwin, 1877

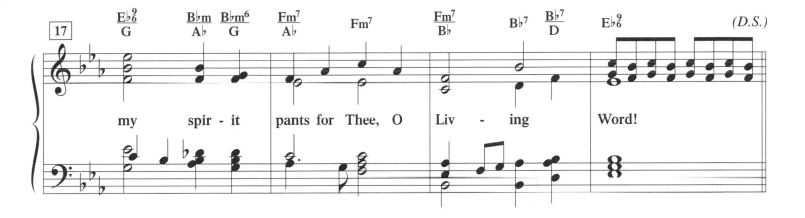

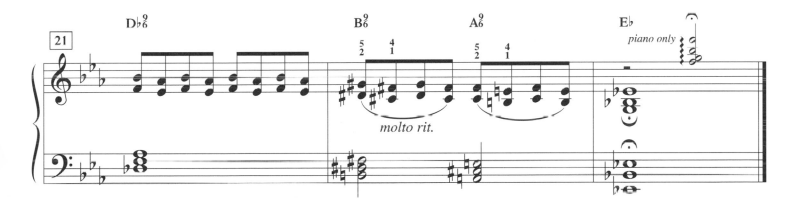

2. Break thou the Bread of Life
   O Lord, to me,
   That hid within my heart
   Thy Word may be.
   Mold Thou each inward thought,
   From self set free,
   And let my steps be all
   Controlled by Thee.

3. Open Thy Word of Truth
   That I may see
   Thy message written clear
   And plain for me.
   Then in sweet fellowship,
   Walking with Thee,
   Thine image on my life
   Engraved will be.

4. O send Thy Spirit, Lord,
   Now unto me,
   That He may touch my eyes
   And make me see.
   Show me the truth concealed
   Within Thy Word;
   And in Thy Book revealed
   I see the Lord.

5. Thou art the Bread of Life
   O Lord, to me,
   Thy holy Word the truth
   That saveth me.
   Give me to eat and live
   With Thee above;
   Teach me to love Thy truth,
   For Thou art love.

6. Bless Thou the truth, dear Lord,
   To me, to me,
   As Thou didst bless the bread
   By Galilee.
   Then shall all bondage cease,
   All fetters fall,
   And I shall find my peace,
   My All in All.

Christ the Lord Is Risen Today

Charles Wesley (1707-1788) and his brother John (1703-1791), sons of an Anglican minister (Samuel), both trained for ministry at Oxford University. While there, they were labeled (somewhat derisively) "methodists" because of the strict regimen of spiritual exercises and scholarship that they developed. After a short unsuccessful stint as missionaries to the Colonies–Georgia, specifically–they returned home to England, frustrated in their spiritual lives. In an interesting parallel to John Newton's life, it was during the sea voyage that seeds were planted, as they watched a group of Moravians experiencing amazing peace during rough seas. Shortly thereafter they experienced spiritual rebirth, and the rest is history–with John's preaching and Charles' hymnwriting becoming the catalyst for a great revival that swept across England. This text, originally 11 stanzas long and sans "alleluias," was introduced in *Hymns and Sacred Poems,* 1739. No one knows who wrote the tune, which had first appeared in *Lyra Davidica,* a hymnal published in 1708 in London. The text and tune were first combined in the *Foundery Collection,* edited in 1742 by John Wesley, at which time the "alleluias" were added.

The Foundry, acquired in 1739 by the Methodists.

EASTER HYMN
Anonymous, 1708

Charles Wesley, 1739

39

2. Lives again our glorious King. Alleluia!
Where, O death, is now thy sting? Alleluia!
Dying once, He all doth save. Alleluia!
Where thy victory, O grave? Alleluia!

3. Love's redeeming work is done. Alleluia!
Fought the fight, the battle won. Alleluia!
Death in vain forbids Him rise. Alleluia!
Christ has opened paradise. Alleluia!

4. Soar we now where Christ has led. Alleluia!
Foll'wing our exalted Head. Alleluia!
Made like Him, like Him we rise. Alleluia!
Ours the cross, the grave, the skies. Alleluia!

FJH2023

Come, Thou Almighty King

This anonymous hymn text first appeared in 1757, in a pamphlet also containing a hymn by Charles Wesley. Its unusual metrical pattern (6.6.4.6.6.6.4) severely limited its choices of available tunes. Initially it was set to a melody which had first appeared 13 years earlier, in 1744, in a collection entitled *Thesaurus Musicus.* That melody, known in the United States as the tune for "My Country, 'Tis of Thee," was originally (and still is today) the setting for "God Save the Queen," the British national anthem. Shortly thereafter, "Come, Thou Almighty King" was reset to a new tune, ITALIAN HYMN, presumably because the original melody contained such political overtones.

The text is an invocation to the Trinity, with stanza one addressed to God the Father, stanza two to God the Son, and stanza three to God the Spirit. Stanza four ties them all together in a summary verse of praise, a doxology. The doctrine of the Trinity is a basic tenet of orthodox Christian faith, and its greatest mystery. On this subject John Wesley once said: "Tell me how it is that in this room there are three candles but one light, and I will explain to you the mode of the divine existence."

Anonymous, ca. 1757

ITALIAN HYMN
Felice de Giardini, 1769

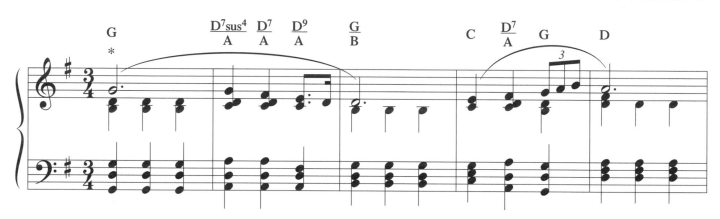

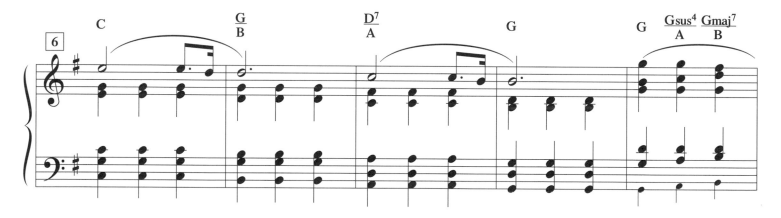

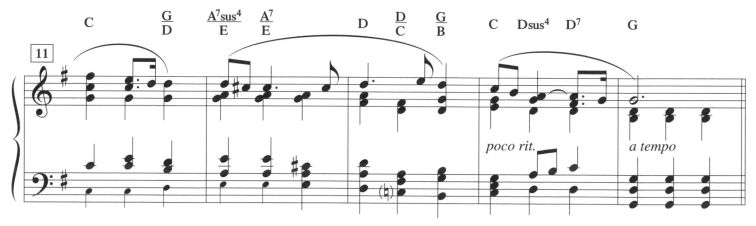

*Quoting G.F. Handel's "Largo" from *Xerxes.*

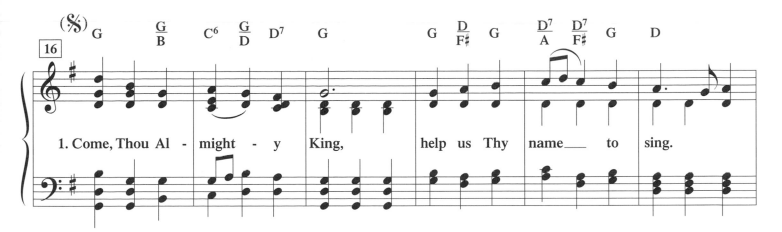

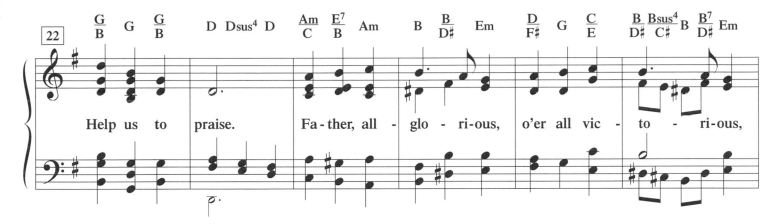

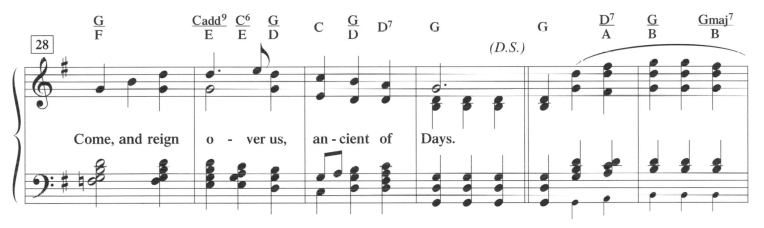

2. Come, Thou Incarnate Word,
Gird on Thy mighty sword.
Our prayer attend.
Come, and Thy people bless,
And give Thy word success.
Spirit of holiness,
On us descend.

3. Come, Holy Comforter,
Thy sacred witness bear
In this glad hour.
Thou, who almighty art,
Now rule in ev'ry heart,
And ne'er from us depart,
Spirit of pow'r.

4. To Thee, great One in Three,
Eternal praises be
Hence evermore.
Thy sov'reign majesty
May we in glory see,
And to eternity
Love and adore.

FJH2023

Come, Thou Fount of Every Blessing

As a youth in London, Robert Robinson (1735-1790) was, by all accounts, destined for failure. Fatherless, he had attached himself to a gang of ruffians who ran the streets. One night in 1752, their "agenda" included heckling the renowned George Whitefield who was speaking nearby. However, as the evangelist preached from the words of John the Baptist in Matthew 3:7 (KJV): "O generation of vipers, who hath warned you to flee from the wrath to come?", Robinson was convicted of his wickedness and that night decided to turn his life around. To make a long story short–six years later, Robinson, now a pastor himself, wrote "Come, Thou Fount of Every Blessing" for the service of Pentecost at his church. A dizzying mixture of metaphors, it is quite possibly the only hymn to ever speak of raising an "Ebenezer!" (According to I Samuel 7:12, this was the name given to a stone monument commemorating God's deliverance of His people, meaning literally, "stone of help.")

Fifty-five years later and an ocean away, the text was first combined with NETTLETON, the anonymous early American tune that is most commonly associated with the hymn today–appearing in John Wyeth's *Repository of Sacred Music, Part Second*, published in 1813.

Robert Robinson, 1758
Stanza 3 alt. 1931

NETTLETON
Traditional American Melody

43

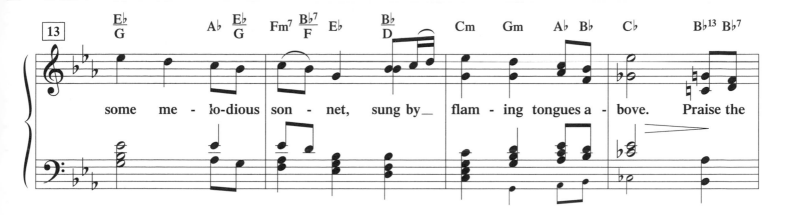

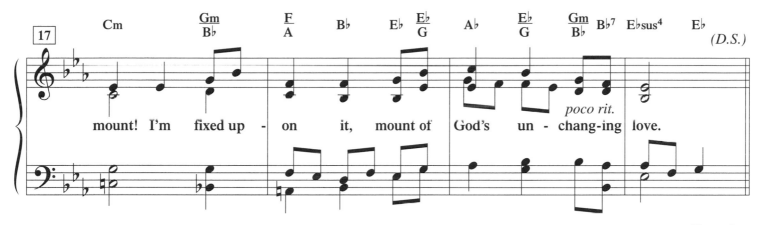

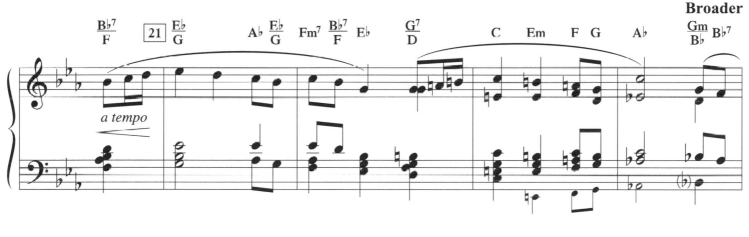

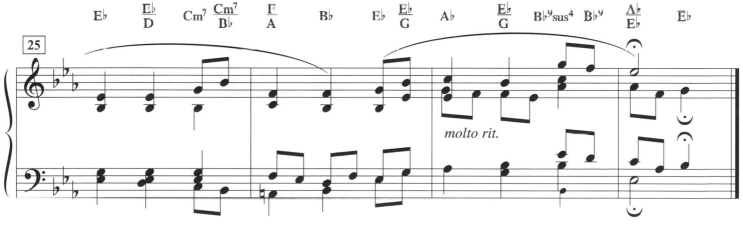

2. Here I raise my Ebenezer;
   Hither by Thy help I'm come.
   And I hope, by Thy good pleasure,
   Safely to arrive at home.
   Jesus sought me when a stranger
   Wand'ring from the fold of God.
   He, to rescue me from danger,
   Interposed His precious blood.

3. Oh, to grace how great a debtor
   Daily I'm constrained to be!
   Let that grace now, like a fetter,
   Bind my yielded heart to Thee.
   Let me know Thee in Thy fullness;
   Guide me by Thy mighty hand
   Till, transformed in Thine own image,
   In Thy presence I shall stand.

Original lyrics–stanza 3, lines 5-8:
Prone to wander, Lord, I feel it,
Prone to leave the God I love.
Here's my heart; Lord, take and seal it,
Seal it for Thy courts above.

FJH2023

Come, Ye Thankful People, Come

Henry Alford was born into an Anglican parsonage in 1810. Following his graduation from Cambridge University, he rose rapidly through the ecclesiastical ranks until he was named dean of Canterbury. His life's work was characterized by careful scholarship and uncommon literary fluency. Among his publications were the volumes *English Descriptive Poetry* and *The Queen's English,* plus several collections of sermons. In a book entitled *A Dissuasive Against Rome,* he rebutted the Oxford Movement in which John Henry Newman and other Anglican ministers converted to Roman Catholicism. But it was his expertise in the Greek language that earned him the greatest distinction in his lifetime. His four-volume *Greek Testament,* on which he labored for 20 years, became the standard New Testament commentary for the latter half of the 19th century. He also wrote a considerable body of poetry, as well as a number of hymns–among them, "Ten Thousand Times Ten Thousand" and "Come, Ye Thankful People, Come."

It is said that Alford harbored a lifelong dream to visit the Holy Land. For whatever reason, whether schedule or health or finances, he never realized that goal. But when he died in 1871 at the age of 61, those who knew of that desire had his tombstone engraved with the Latin inscription: *Deversorium viatoris proficientis Hierosolymam,* "the inn of a pilgrim traveling to Jerusalem." How fitting for a devout servant of God who never let his strenuous earthly duties obscure his vision of the New Jerusalem!

George J. Elvey (1816-1893) composed the tune ST. GEORGE'S, WINDSOR, which has become the setting of choice for "Come, Ye Thankful People, Come." Elvey served for 47 years as organist at the historic royal chapel at Windsor Castle. In 1871 he was knighted by Queen Victoria for his many years of faithful service to the royal family and also for his various musical compositions–including several oratorios, anthems, and collections of service music. Besides ST. GEORGES, WINDSOR, Elvey is remembered today for his tune DIADEMATA, most commonly associated with the text "Crown Him with Many Crowns."

ST. GEORGE'S WINDSOR

Henry Alford, 1844

George J. Elvey, 1858

2. All the world is God's own field,
Fruit unto His praise to yield;
Wheat and tares together sown,
Unto joy or sorrow grown.
First the blade, and then the ear,
Then the full corn shall appear.
Lord of harvest, grant that we
Wholesome grain and pure may be.

3. For the Lord our God shall come,
And shall take His harvest home;
From His field shall in that day
All offenses purge away;
Give His angels charge at last
In the fire the tares to cast,
But the fruitful ears to store
In His garner evermore.

4. Even so, Lord, quickly come
To Thy final harvest home;
Gather Thou Thy people in,
Free from sorrows, free from sin;
There forever purified,
In Thy presence to abide.
Come, with all Thine angels come;
Raise the glorious harvest home.

Crown Him with Many Crowns

Matthew Bridges (1800-1894) was an English poet and writer who published, among other things, two collections of hymns. His 1852 volume, *In the Passion of Jesus*, contained a text that he had written the year before: "Crown Him with Many Crowns." Godfrey Thring (1823-1903) was rector of two obscure rural parishes in the south of England. Due to the idyllic nature of his pastoral duties there, he had plenty of time to write hymns and compile hymnals. His 1874 collection–*Hymns and Sacred Lyrics*–included "Crown Him with Many Crowns," altered somewhat with at least one more stanza added, and united with the DIADEMATA tune recently composed by George J. Elvey (1816-1893).

Elvey served for 47 years as organist at the historic royal chapel at Windsor Castle. In 1871 he was knighted by Queen Victoria for his many years of faithful service to the royal family and also for his various musical compositions–including several oratorios, anthems, and collections of service music. Besides DIADEMATA, Elvey is remembered today for his tune ST. GEORGE'S, WINDSOR, most commonly associated with the text "Come, Ye Thankful People, Come."

Matthew Bridges, 1851
Alt. by Godfrey Thring, 1874

DIADEMATA
George J. Elvey, 1868

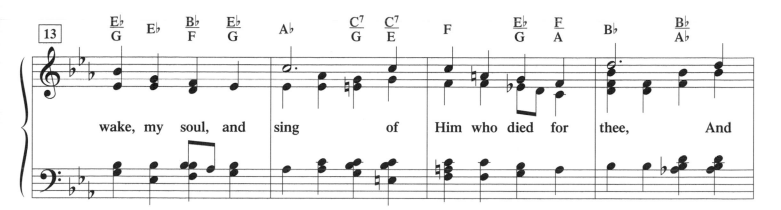

wake, my soul, and sing of Him who died for thee, And

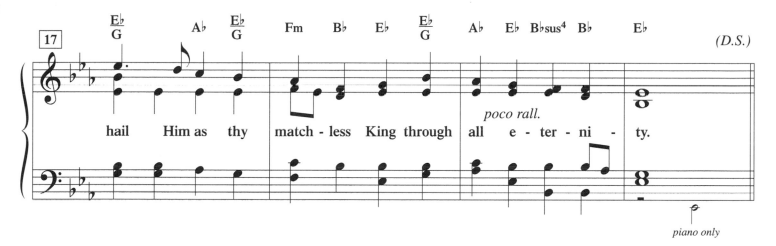

hail Him as thy match-less King through all e-ter-ni-ty.

poco rall.

(D.S.)

piano only

Slightly broader

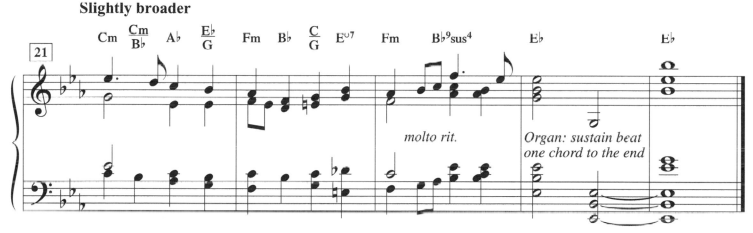

molto rit.

Organ: sustain beat one chord to the end

2. Crown Him the Lord of Love!
   Behold His hands and side,
   Rich wounds, yet visible above,
   In beauty glorified.
   No angel in the sky
   Can fully bear that sight,
   But downward bends his wond'ring eyes
   At mysteries so bright.

3. Crown Him the Lord of Peace!
   Whose pow'r a scepter sways
   From pole to pole that wars may cease,
   Absorbed in prayer and praise.
   His reign shall know no end;
   And round His pierced feet
   Fair flowers of paradise extend
   Their fragrance ever sweet.

4. Crown Him the Lord of Years,
   The Potentate of Time,
   Creator of the rolling spheres,
   Ineffably sublime.
   All hail, Redeemer, hail!
   For Thou hast died for me;
   Thy praise and glory shall not fail
   Throughout eternity.

5. Crown Him the Lord of Life!
   Who triumphed o'er the grave;
   Who rose victorious to the strife
   For those He came to save.
   His glories now we sing
   Who died and rose on high,
   Who died eternal life to bring,
   And lives that death may die.

6. Crown Him the Lord of Heav'n!
   One with the Father known,
   One with the Spirit through Him giv'n
   From yonder glorious throne.
   To Thee be endless praise,
   For Thou for us hast died.
   Be Thou, O Lord, through endless days
   Adored and magnified.

Fairest Lord Jesus

"Schoenster Herr Jesu" was an anonymous German hymn text which first appeared in the Roman Catholic hymnal, *Münster Gesangbuch,* published in 1677. As the hymn spread across Germany for the next 162 years, mainly by oral tradition, it experienced minor changes to its text and somehow became wedded to the Silesian folktune that we know today. In 1839, Hoffman von Fallersleben heard the hymn for the first time and transcribed it as it had evolved to that point. Three years later he included it in his 1842 songbook, *Schlesische Volkslieder (Silesian Folksongs).* In 1850, Richard S. Willis arranged the harmony as we know it today, and published the hymn with an anonymous English translation in his *Church Chorals and Choir Studies,* thus introducing it to American worshippers. Willis' footnote to the hymn stated that it was originally sung by German pilgrims on their way to Jerusalem during the Crusades of the 12th century. This perception was propagated by no less than Franz Lizst, who incorporated the tune into his oratorio, *The Legend of St. Elizabeth.* In the appendix to the full score, he states that he had received the tune and text from an old cantor named Gottschalg who had told him that it was "an old pilgrim song apparently from the Crusades." Based on this legend, the tune name is often listed in hymnals as CRUSADERS' HYMN. However, recent hymnologists have expressed doubt that the text goes back more than a few years before its first appearance in 1677, nor the tune much before the 18th century, due to lack of evidence to the contrary. In 1873, Joseph A. Seiss created an alternate translation from German to English, resulting in a hymn text known as "Beautiful Savior." Today's hymnals generally contain a combination of the two translations.

CRUSADERS' HYMN
Silesian Folksong

Anonymous German Hymn

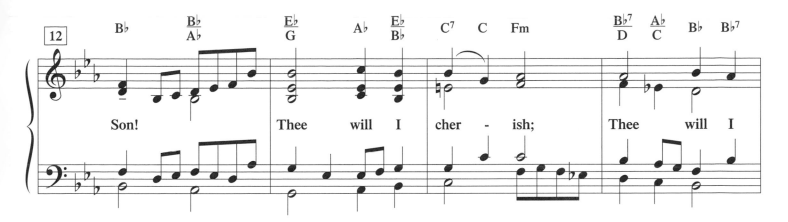

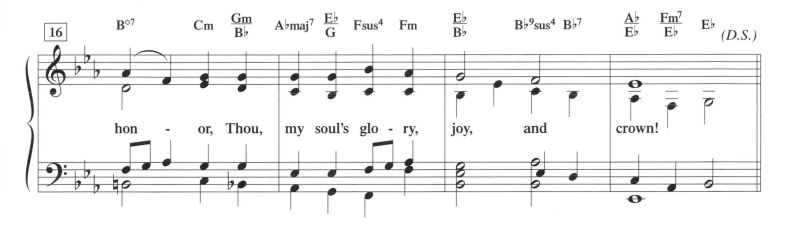

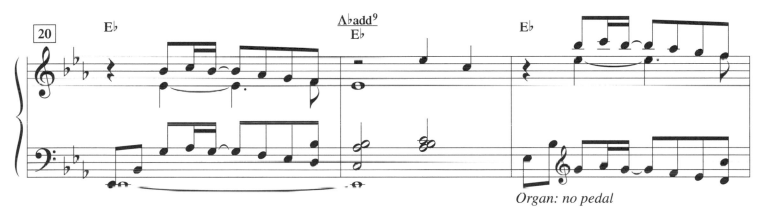

Organ: no pedal

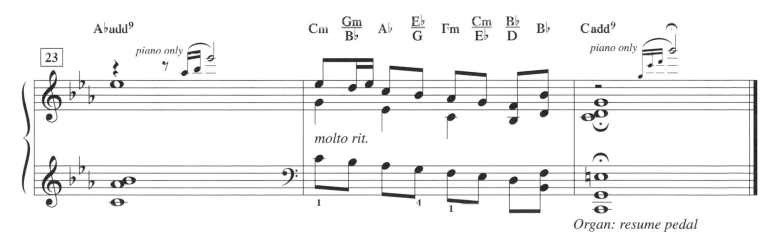

Organ: resume pedal

2. Fair are the meadows;
Fairer still the woodlands,
Robed in the blooming garb of spring.
Jesus is fairer;
Jesus is purer,
Who makes the woeful heart to sing!

3. Fair is the sunshine;
Fairer still the moonlight,
And all the twinkling starry host.
Jesus shines brighter;
Jesus shines purer
Than all the angels heav'n can boast.

4. Beautiful Savior!
Lord of all the nations!
Son of God and Son of man!
Glory and honor,
Praise, adoration,
Now and forevermore be Thine!

Faith of Our Fathers

Frederick William Faber, son of an English clergyman, was born at Yorkshire in 1814. Educated at Balliol College and Oxford University, he was ordained a minister in the Anglican Church in 1843. However, while at Oxford, he had been influenced by John Henry Newman, leader of what had come to be known as the Oxford Movement, and in 1846 he switched his loyalties to the Roman Church. For most of his career, he labored alongside Newman in the Catholic church of St. Philip Neri in London. A talented writer, he published several books of prose and three volumes of hymns. It's interesting to note that he limited his output of hymns to 150, following the example of an ancient gnostic who propagated his doctrines through the same number of hymns as are found in the Old Testament Book of Psalms. Most of Faber's best hymns were published in a volume called *Jesus and Mary*–obviously written from a Catholic perspective. As a matter of fact, his best-known hymn–"Faith of Our Fathers"–originally contained the lines, "Faith of our fathers! Mary's prayers shall win this country back to Thee," thus expressing the hope that England would someday be brought back to the papal fold. Faber is also remembered for writing "There's a Wideness in God's Mercy." He died at the age of 49, in 1863.

ST. CATHERINE
Henri F. Hemy, 1864

Frederick W. Faber, 1849

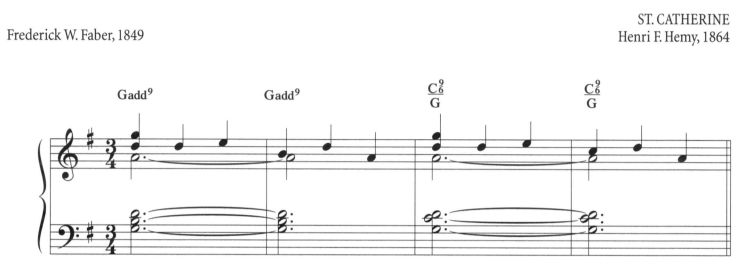

Organ option: on first system, play top notes of treble clef on chimes; play the bass clef on different manual

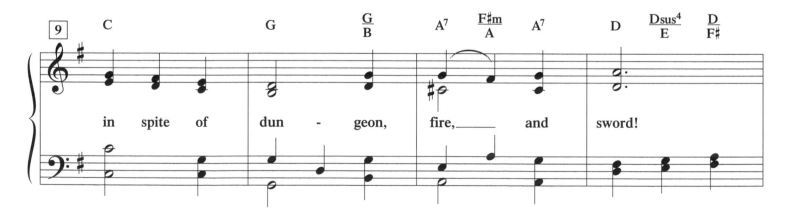

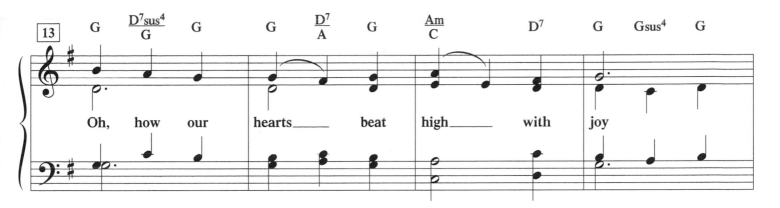

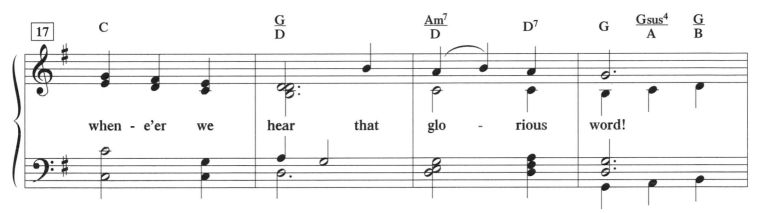

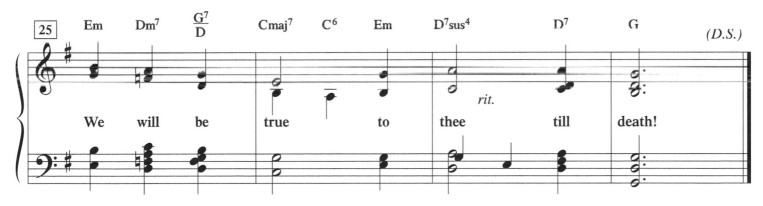

2. Our fathers, chained in prisons dark,
   Were still in heart and conscience free.
   How sweet would be their children's fate
   If they, like them, could die for thee!
   Faith of our fathers! holy faith!
   We will be true to thee till death!

3. Faith of our fathers! we will strive
   To win all nations unto thee;
   And through the truth that comes from God,
   Mankind shall then be truly free.
   Faith of our fathers! holy faith!
   We will be true to thee till death!

4. Faith of our fathers! we will love
   Both friend and foe in all our strife,
   And preach thee, too, as love knows how,
   By kindly words and virtuous life.
   Faith of our fathers! holy faith!
   We will be true to thee till death!

For All the Saints

William Walsham How was born into a wealthy English family in 1823. After receiving his ministerial training at Oxford, he was ordained by the Anglican church. His sermons were regularly punctuated by stirring poetry from his own pen–snippets from the approximately 60 hymns that he wrote in his lifetime. In 1864, How collaborated with John Ellerton to publish the collection *Church Hymns.* Among How's inclusions in the project were two hymns still in use today: "For All the Saints" and "O Word of God Incarnate." (Other How contributions to modern hymnody include "We Give Thee But Thine Own" and "O Jesus, Thou Art Standing.") In 1879, Queen Victoria appointed him Bishop of Bedford at his request, making the slums of East London his diocese. There he became known as the "omnibus bishop" because he eschewed the private coach which would normally have been one of the perks of his position, opting instead to ride in public transportation along with his poverty-stricken parishioners. The beloved pastor died in 1897, leaving behind a legacy of meaningful hymns and humble service on behalf of the poor.

When the so-called high church wing of the Church of England published *The English Hymnal* in 1906, their music editor–the brilliant composer, Ralph Vaughan Williams (1872-1958)–composed the melody SINE NOMINE as a setting for How's stirring All Saints' Day hymn text. Some have speculated that the tune name–Latin for "without name"–was a humorous jab at the custom of giving hymn tunes names of their own. However, it's more likely a reflection of the fact that all of the thousands of saints alluded to the text are unnamed–in contrast to such places as Hebrews 11 in scripture, or the Westminster Abbey in London, where the honored dead are individually named and memorialized.

SINE NOMINE

William W. How, 1864

Ralph Vaughan Williams, 1906

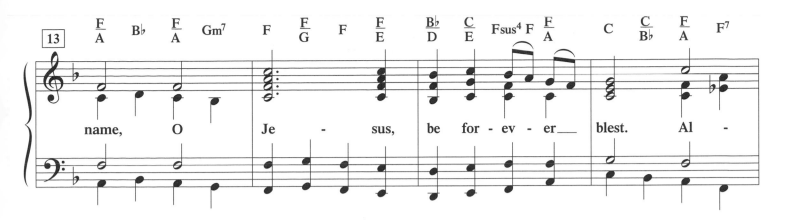

name, O Je - sus, be for - ev - er___ blest. Al -

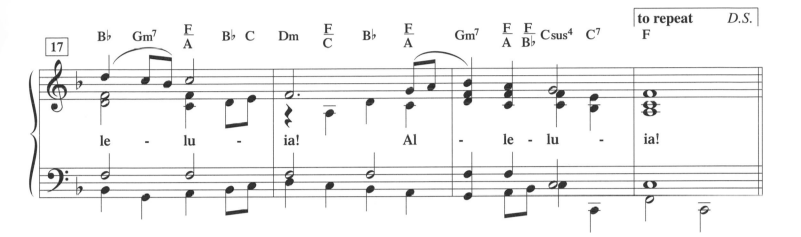

to repeat   D.S.

le - lu - ia!   Al - le - lu - ia!

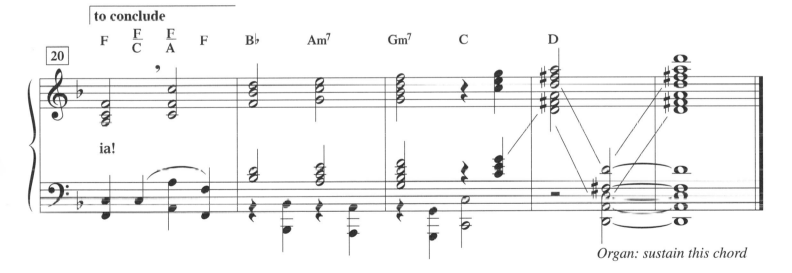

to conclude

ia!

Organ: sustain this chord

2. Thou wast their Rock, their Fortress, and their Might;
   Thou, Lord, their Captain in the well-fought fight;
   Thou, in the darkness drear, their one true Light.
   Alleluia! Alleluia!

3. Oh, may Thy soldiers, faithful, true, and bold,
   Fight as the saints who nobly fought of old,
   And win with them the victor's crown of gold.
   Alleluia! Alleluia!

4. Oh, blest communion, fellowship divine!
   We feebly struggle; they in glory shine.
   Yet all are one in Thee, for all are Thine.
   Alleluia! Alleluia!

5. But lo! there breaks a yet more glorious day:
   The saints triumphant rise in bright array;
   The King of Glory passes on His way.
   Alleluia! Alleluia!

6. From earth's wide bounds, from ocean's farthest coast,
   Through gates of pearl streams in the countless host,
   Singing to Father, Son, and Holy Ghost:
   Alleluia! Alleluia!

For the Beauty of the Earth

Folliott Sandford Pierpoint (1835-1917), an Englishman, received his degree at Cambridge. A lifelong educator, he was the classical master at Somersetshire College and a regular contributor to sacred poetry journals. His most famous hymn, "For the Beauty of the Earth," first appeared in the 1864 collection, *Lyra Eucharista*. Originally, the last two lines were:

> *Christ, our God, to Thee we raise*
> *This our sacrifice of praise.*

While the current version flows better, it misses Pierpoint's reminder that the Bible often refers to singing as a sacrifice–either a "sacrifice of praise" or a "sacrifice of joy." Hebrews 13:15 exhorts: "By him (Jesus Christ) therefore, let us offer the sacrifice of praise to God continually, that is, the fruit of our lips giving thanks to his name."

The tune, originally known as TREUER HEILAND, had been written in 1838 by the German, Conrad Kocher (1786-1872). It became known as DIX because of its association with "As with Gladness Men of Old," written ca. 1858 by William Chatterton Dix (who is perhaps best remembered as the author of "What Child Is This").

DIX

Folliott S. Pierpoint, 1864

Conrad Kocher, 1838

Glorious Things of Thee Are Spoken

John Newton was born in London in 1725. His mother was a quiet, devout woman and his father was an austere shipmaster who was rarely home. As a young lad, John was taught the basics of the Christian faith at the knee of his mother, whom he adored. But when he was seven she died from tuberculosis, and John's idyllic world came crashing in, leading to a tumultuous and rebellious childhood. After a couple of apprenticeships as a sailor, during which time John strayed from the faith, he was impressed into the British navy at the age of 20. Finding the conditions deplorable, he deserted. Arrested two days later, he was flogged and then transferred to duty on a slave ship. At this point he was a rabid atheist, and "exceedingly vile," as he later confessed. For two years his life spiraled downward, finally reaching rock bottom as he himself became the servant of an abusive slave trader in Sierra Leone. His father, knowing that he was involved in this nefarious business but having lost track of his whereabouts, put out the request to ship owners to find him and bring him home. Providentially, the captain of the slave ship *Greyhound* crossed paths with him and allowed him to board the vessel for the long journey back to England by way of Brazil. Out of sheer boredom, Newton picked up Thomas á Kempis' *The Imitation of Christ.* Though it disturbed him greatly, wicked as he was, it nevertheless planted seeds in his mind. Later that same voyage, a violent storm nearly sank the ship, bringing Newton to his knees. Surviving the storm, he continued in the slave trade for another four years. However, the trauma of that journey had set events in motion that would eventually transform Newton into a minister of the Gospel, a social reformer, and a hymn writer. "Glorious Things of Thee Are Spoken" is probably his second most famous hymn, written in 1779, the same year that he wrote his most famous one, "Amazing Grace."

Throughout his long life, he teamed up with men like William Wilberforce and John Wesley to crusade against slavery. Finally, in March of 1807, Parliament passed Wilberforce's bill abolishing the British slave trade. Later that same year, the 82-yr-old Newton died. His last words: "I am a great sinner...and Christ is a great Savior."

AUSTRIAN HYMN

John Newton, 1779

Franz Joseph Haydn, 1797

2. See, the streams of living waters,
Springing from eternal Love,
Well supply thy sons and daughters,
And all fear of want remove.
Who can faint while such a river
Ever flows, their thirst to assuage?
Grace which, like the Lord, the Giver,
Never fails from age to age!

3. Round each habitation hovering,
See the cloud and fire appear
For a glory and a covering,
Showing that the Lord is near!
Thus they march, the pillar leading,
Light by night and shade by day,
Daily on the manna feeding
Which He gives them when they pray.

4. Savior, since of Zion's city
I through grace a member am,
Let the world deride or pity–
I will glory in Thy name.
Fading is the world's best pleasure,
All its boasted pomp and show;
Solid joys and lasting treasures
None but Zion's children know.

Go, Tell It on the Mountain

*The Africans who were brought to the American South on slave ships were very musical people, accustomed to expressing religious ideas in song. Sometimes they would pick up pieces of hymns or biblical text–perhaps by waiting outside the churches–and would incorporate these words and melodies into their songs. The slaves would sing while working all day, and then would often meet at night, sometimes secretly for fear of punishment, where they would improvise in song and dance for hours, even after a hard day's work. These were songs of survival, songs that gave the courage to go on living when life seemed to be nothing but pain. Biblical stories such as Daniel in the lions' den, the Israelites' slavery in Egypt, and the birth of a Messiah–they all spoke powerful messages of hope to those who were oppressed. Sometimes the songs were created as a way of pouring out to God their deepest prayers, desires, and frustrations. They were created all throughout the 200 years of slavery, although they weren't known to most Americans until the latter half of the 19th century.

"Go, Tell It on the Mountain" is one of these "spirituals"–as they became known–which has taken its place in standard hymnody. Probably dating from the early 1800s, it was first popularized in 1879 by the Fisk University Jubilee Singers. This outstanding choir toured the United States and Europe, representing the school which had been founded to educate freed slaves. While raising money for their scholarship fund, they introduced a new genre of music to much of the world. In 1907, John Work, Jr. added the stanzas. In 1940 his son, John Work III, made an editorial decision regarding the different variations on the melody in the refrain, creating the definitive arrangement still used in many hymnals today. (The arrangement below is based on his version of the melody.)

Refrain: Traditional Spiritual
Stanzas: John Work, Jr., 1907

GO TELL IT
Traditional Spiritual

*First paragraph from the foreword in Teresa Wilhelmi's FJH piano collection, *Poor Wayfaring Stranger*, FF1424.

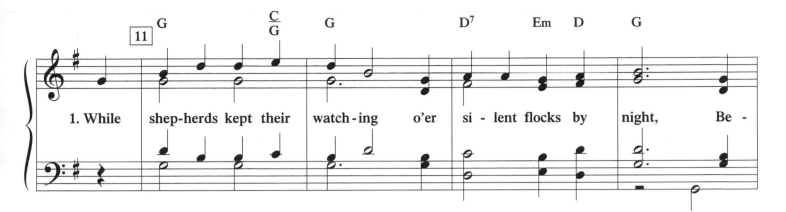

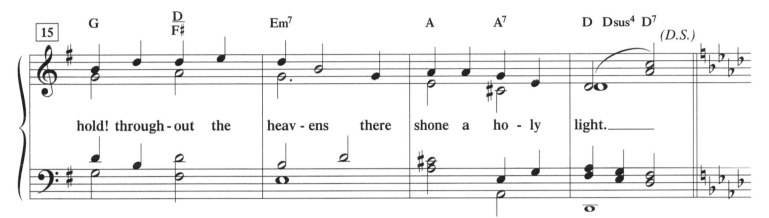

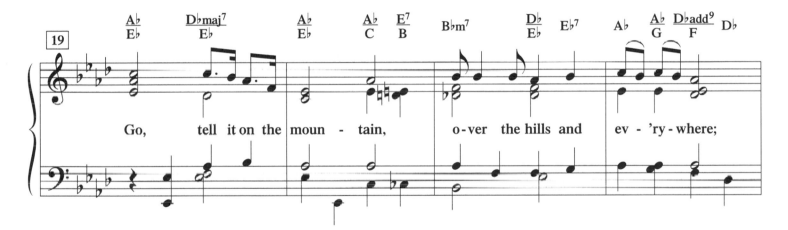

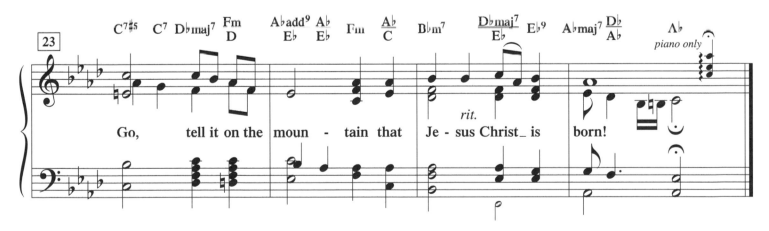

2. The shepherds feared and trembled
   When lo! above the earth
   Rang out the angel chorus
   That hailed our Savior's birth.

   Go, tell it...

3. Down in a lowly manger
   The humble Christ was born,
   And brought us God's salvation
   That blessed Christmas morn.

   Go, tell it...

Good Christian Men, Rejoice

During the Middle Ages, the Roman Mass included no congregational singing–but only Gregorian chants sung in Latin. The "barbarian languages" used in everyday conversation were considered too crude for use in church music–or any aspect of worship, for that matter. The carol known today as "Good Christian Men, Rejoice" began as a Latin poem written sometime in the 14th century. That poem, which started with the line "In dulci jubilo," was set to an anonymous German tune in 1601 by one Bartholomaeus Gesius.

John Mason Neale (1818-1866) was a minister in the Church of England. Caught up in the Oxford Movement, he became interested in the original languages–specifically, Greek and Latin–that had cradled the early liturgies of the Church. He became a renowned translator of ancient hymns–among them, "All Glory, Laud, and Honor," "Of the Father's Love Begotten," "O Come, O Come, Emmanuel, and "Good Christian Men, Rejoice."

Latin Carol, 14th century
Tr. by John M. Neale, 1855

IN DULCI JUBILO
Traditional German Carol, 14th century

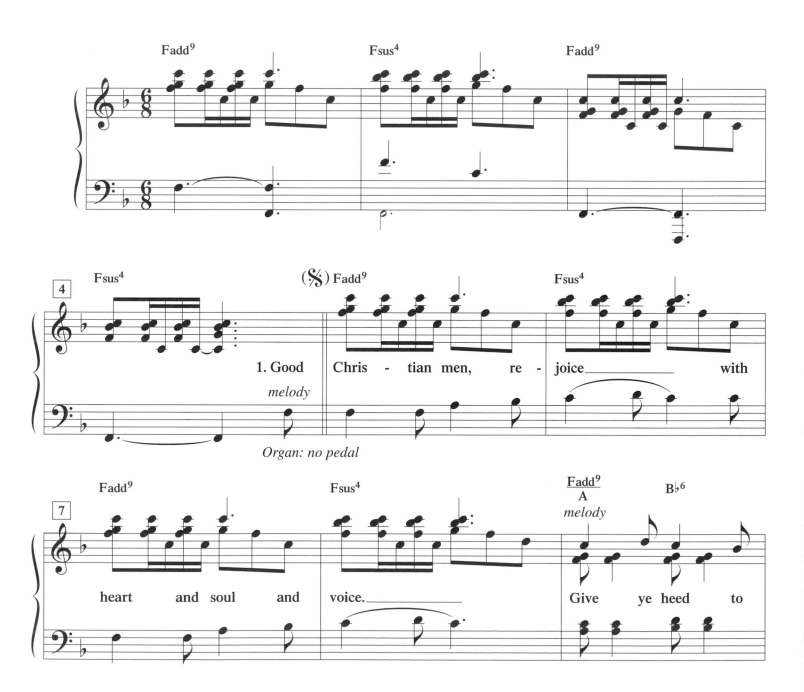

2. Good Christian men, rejoice
   With heart and soul and voice.
   Now ye hear of endless bliss:
   Joy! Joy! Jesus Christ was born for this.
   He hath opened heaven's door
   And man is blessed forevermore.
   Christ was born for this!
   Christ was born for this!

3. Good Christian men, rejoice
   With heart and soul and voice.
   Now ye need not fear the grave:
   Peace! Peace! Jesus Christ was born to save.
   Calls you one and calls you all
   To gain His everlasting hall.
   Christ was born to save!
   Christ was born to save!

FJH2023

Great Is Thy Faithfulness

Thomas O. Chisholm (1866-1960) was an American by birth, a Methodist by rebirth, and a life insurance agent by career choice. As an avocation, he wrote religious poetry, often sending it to his friend and collaborator, William M. Runyan (1870-1957). Their best known hymn, "Great Is Thy Faithfulness," written in 1923, was inspired by two scriptures: "His compassions fail not. They are new every morning; great is thy faithfulness" (Lam. 3:22-23) and "Every good gift and every perfect gift is from above, and cometh down from the Father of lights, with whom is no variableness, neither shadow of turning" (James 1:17). The hymn was a favorite of Dr. Will Houghton, president of Moody Bible Institute in Chicago, Illinois, where it was often sung in the chapel services, thus earning a place in the hearts of hundreds of ministerial students. In addition, it was often featured on the Institute's radio station, WMBI, in programs like "Hymns from the Chapel," featuring the artistry of George Beverly Shea, vocalist, and Don Hustad, organist. In 1954, Shea introduced the hymn to British audiences during a series of crusades by a young evangelist named Billy Graham, and it quickly became a favorite there too.

FAITHFULNESS

Thomas O. Chisholm, 1923

William M. Runyan, 1923

Organ: no pedal

63

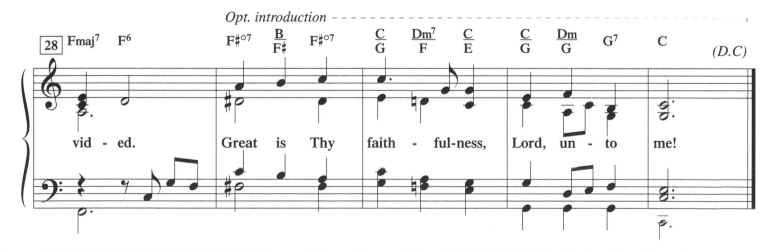

2. Summer and winter and springtime and harvest,
Sun, moon, and stars in their courses above,
Join with all nature in manifold witness
To Thy great faithfulness, mercy, and love.
Great is Thy faithfulness...

3. Pardon for sin and a peace that endureth,
Thy own dear presence to cheer and to guide,
Strength for today and bright hope for tomorrow—
Blessings all mine, with ten thousand beside!
Great is Thy faithfulness...

FJH2023

Guide Me, O Thou Great Jehovah

William Williams was born in Wales in 1717. He originally intended to enter the medical profession. However, a spiritual crisis in his life turned him toward the ministry, and after some time he was ordained a deacon in the Church of England. Denied full ordination because of his nonconformist tendencies, he identified himself with the Wesley brothers and their itinerent evangelistic techniques. After a short time he found himself in disagreement with their doctrine of free grace though, and so organized what could best be described as a Calvinistic Methodist movement, with all of Wales as his parish. Like the Wesleys, he traveled by horseback, logging some 100,000 miles over 45 years, preaching wherever the opportunity arose. And like the Wesleys, he was occasionally roughed up or heckled by young rowdies. In addition, like the Wesleys, he wrote hymns–an estimated 800 in his lifetime–to summarize and accentuate his sermons. Affectionately known as "the sweet singer of Wales," his effect on hymnody in his own country was similar to that of the Wesleys and Isaac Watts in England, and that of Luther in Germany. His first hymn collection, *Hallellujah,* was published in 1744. His only hymn still widely used today, "Guide Me, O Thou Great Jehovah," was originally written in Welsh. When he and Peter Williams (no relation) later translated it into English in 1771, it was entitled "Strength to Pass Through the Wilderness." A study of its text reveals many allusions to the 40-year journey of the Israelites from Egypt to the Promised Land, with wider applications to the life of all Christian pilgrims on their way to the "new Promised Land."

The Welsh people have long been known for their enthusiastic singing. Welsh coal miners often sang on their way to work in the deep tunnels. When spiritual revivals have periodically swept the country during the past 250 years, usually the hymn singing has been a greater catalyst than the preaching. Many of the strongest and most interesting tunes in modern hymnals have come out of this small country nestled against England. And still today, they sing "Guide Me, O Thou Great Jehovah" at the beginning of outdoor athletic events, just as many countries sing a national anthem.

William Williams, 1745
Tr. by William Williams and Peter Williams, 1771

CWM RHONDDA
John Hughes, 1907

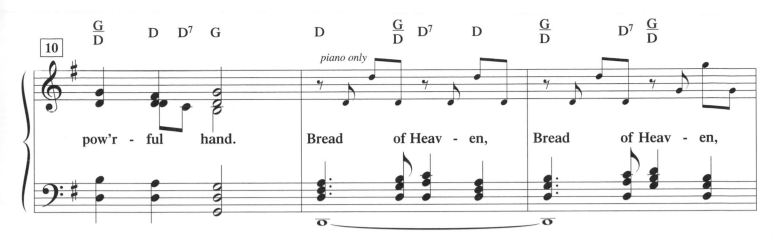

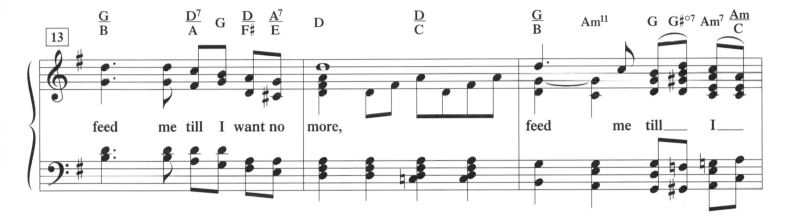

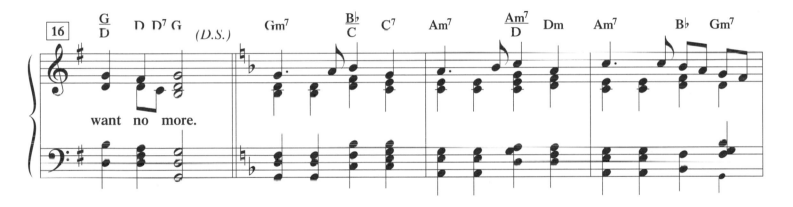

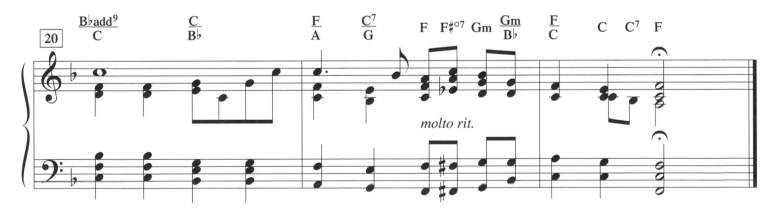

2. Open now the crystal fountain
   Whence the healing stream doth flow.
   Let the fire and cloudy pillar
   Lead me all my journey through.
   Strong Deliverer, strong Deliverer,
   Be Thou still my Strength and Shield,
   Be Thou still my Strength and Shield.

3. When I tread the verge of Jordan,
   Bid my anxious fears subside.
   Death of death, and hell's destruction,
   Land me safe on Canaan's side.
   Songs of praises, songs of praises
   I will ever give to Thee,
   I will ever give to Thee.

Hark! the Herald Angels Sing

Besides being preachers and social reformers, the brothers John and Charles Wesley made enormous contributions to English hymnody. (See "Christ the Lord Is Risen Today" for more details on their background.) John wrote a few hymns himself, but mainly translated Moravian hymns from German and edited hymnbooks. Charles, on the other hand, wrote almost 9,000 poems, of which some 6,500 were hymn texts. In 1739 their third hymn collection was published, entitled *Hymns and Sacred Poems*. It included, among others, a poem by Charles entitled "Hark How All the Welkin (an archaic term for 'sky') Rings." As with many of the hymnbooks of that time, there was no music included–only the poetic meter so that the hymn text could be wed to appropriate tunes passed along by oral tradition. During subsequent years, the hymn text was altered and modified by a succession of editors (including their colleague, George Whitefield) as it found its way into other collections. However it languished as only a moderately popular hymn for over a century.

In 1840, Felix Mendelssohn composed a cantata entitled *Festgesang (Festival Song)* for a Leipzig celebration of the 400th anniversary of Gutenberg's invention of printing with moveable type. Sixteen years later, William H. Cummings, organist at Waltham Abbey (and a Mendelssohn enthusiast) made a happy discovery: it occurred to him that the melody of the second chorus of *Festgesang*–"Gott Ist Licht" (God Is Light)–would be a suitable vehicle for the stirring Wesley Christmas text which continued to show up in hymnals, but wedded to inferior tunes. He adapted the lyrics from their original form of ten four-line stanzas to the form we know today: four eight-line stanzas. In addition, he added the short refrain in order to make the text fit the music. This excellent new setting was included the very next year, 1857, in Richard Chope's *Congregational Hymn and Tune Book*. From there it quickly became one the most celebrated carols in the world.

Charles Wesley, 1739

MENDELSSOHN
Felix Mendelssohn, 1840
Adapted by William H. Cummings, 1856

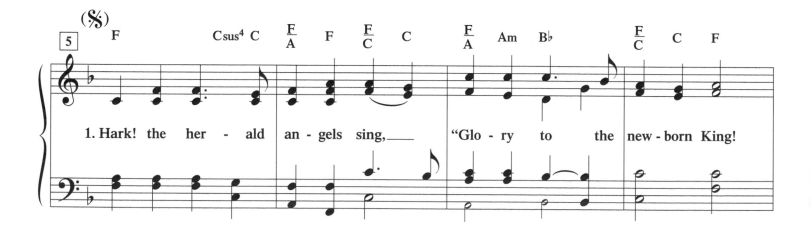

2. Christ, by highest heav'n adored!
   Christ, the everlasting Lord!
   Long desired, behold Him come,
   Offspring of the Virgin's womb.
   Veiled in flesh the Godhead see;
   Hail th'incarnate Deity,
   Pleased as man with men to dwell,
   Jesus, our Immanuel!
   Hark! the herald angels sing,
   "Glory to the newborn King."

3. Hail, the heav'n-born Prince of Peace!
   Hail, the Sun of Righteousness!
   Light and life to all He brings,
   Ris'n with healing in His wings.
   Mild He lays His glory by,
   Born that man no more may die,
   Born to raise the sons of earth,
   Born to give them second birth.
   Hark! the herald angels sing,
   "Glory to the newborn King."

FJH2023

Holy, Holy, Holy! Lord God Almighty

Reginald Heber, born in England in 1783, was educated at Oxford University. Following his ordination in the Church of England, he served in a small parish for 16 years, during which time he wrote many hymns and developed a modest amount of fame through these and other literary activities. One hymn written during this time, "From Greenland's Icy Mountains," reflected the desire for missionary service which burned in his heart. In 1822, this prayer was answered, and Heber was appointed Bishop of Calcutta, where he ordained the first Indian pastor of the Episcopal Church. However, the rigorous environment proved to be detrimental to his health and he died a few years later. But fortunately for the Christian Church universal, he lived long enough to pen the immortal text, "Holy, Holy, Holy! Lord God Almighty," in 1826, the year of his death. The tune which has been inextricably linked to this text was written years later by John Bacchus Dykes, precentor of Durham Cathedral. A glance at the index of composers in most hymnals will reveal the major impact that Dykes has had on Christian hymnody, with some of his other tunes including MELITA ("Eternal Father, Strong to Save") and ST. AGNES ("Jesus, the Very Thought of Thee").

NICAEA
John B. Dykes, 1861

Reginald Heber, 1826

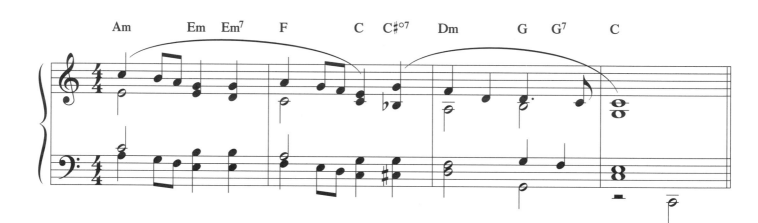

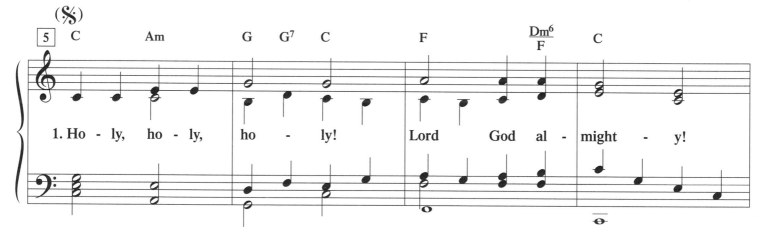

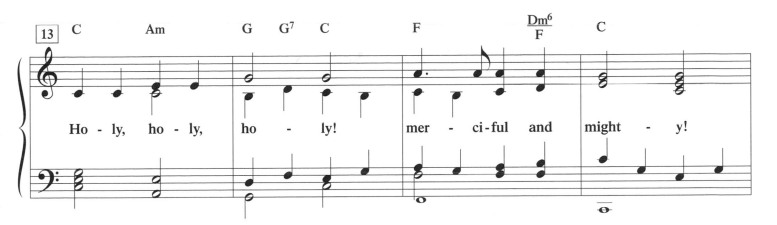

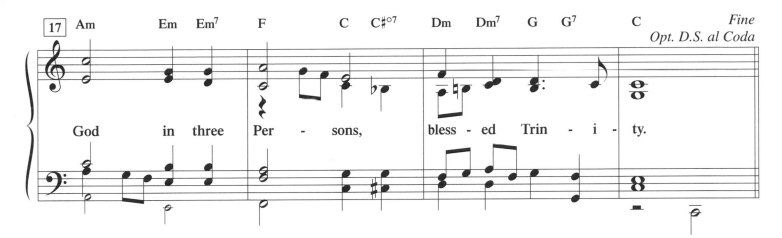

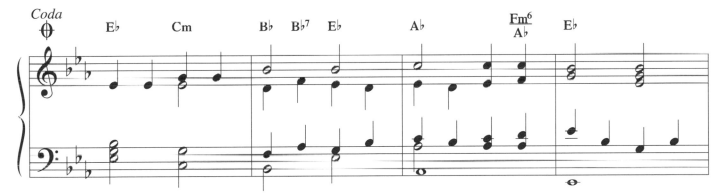

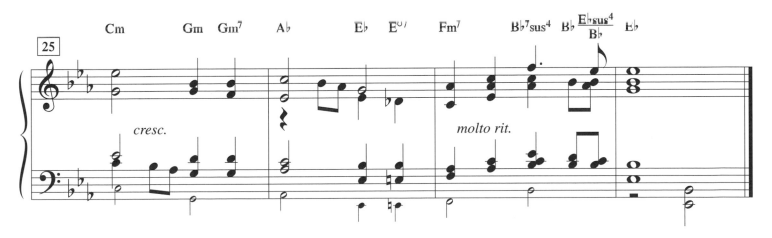

2. Holy, holy, holy! all the saints adore Thee,
   Casting down their golden crowns around the glassy sea;
   Cherubim and seraphim falling down before Thee,
   Which wert, and art, and evermore shalt be.

3. Holy, holy, holy! though the darkness hide Thee,
   Though the eye of sinful man Thy glory may not see;
   Only Thou art holy–there is none beside Thee
   Perfect in pow'r, in love, in purity.

4. Holy, holy, holy! Lord God Almighty!
   All Thy works shall praise Thy name in earth, and sky, and sea.
   Holy, holy, holy! merciful and mighty!
   God in three Persons, blessed Trinity!

FJH2023

How Firm a Foundation

In 1787, an English Baptist minister named John Rippon compiled a hymnal with the less-than-catchy title, *A Selection of Hymns.* Included was a text, the authorship of which was documented only by the signature "K____". Originally entitled "How Firm a Foundation, Ye Saints of the Lord," that text has since appeared in nearly every major hymnal to this present day. At least three names have been considered as the author–Kirkham, Keith, and Keen–with modern scholarship leaning toward the latter, though nothing is known concerning this person.

The first stanza reminds Christians that God's written Word is the foundation for their faith. The remaining stanzas are enclosed in quotation marks, indicating that they are promises extracted directly from scripture, set in metrical form. For example, stanza 2 comes from Isaiah 41:10 (KJV): "Fear thou not, for I am with thee; be not dismayed, for I am thy God. I will strengthen thee, yea, I will help thee. Yea, I will uphold thee with the right hand of my righteousness."

The tune FOUNDATION is anonymous, first appearing in Caldwell's *Union Harmony,* published in the United States in 1837.

FOUNDATION
Traditional American Melody

Anonymous

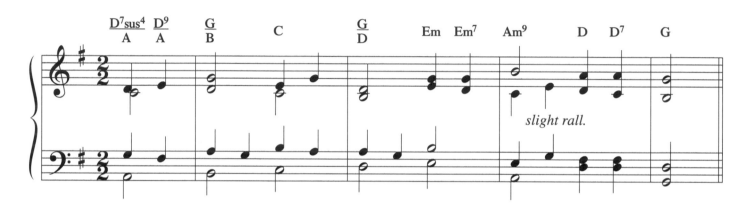

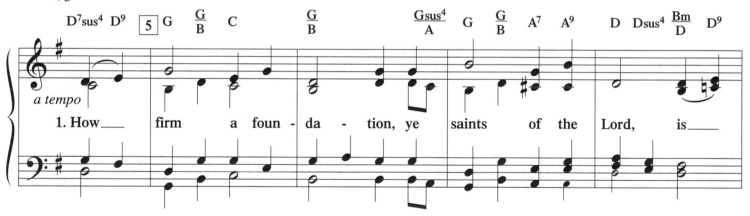

Organ: no pedal

2. "Fear not; I am with thee. O be not dismayed,
   For I am thy God; I will still give thee aid.
   I'll strengthen thee, help thee, and cause thee to stand,
   Upheld by My gracious omnipotent hand."

3. "When through the deep waters I call thee to go,
   The rivers of sorrow shall not overflow;
   For I will be with thee, thy trials to bless,
   And sanctify to thee thy deepest distress."

4. "When through fiery trials thy pathway shall lie,
   My grace all-sufficient shall be thy supply.
   The flames shall not hurt thee; I only design
   Thy dross to consume and thy gold to refine."

5. "The soul that on Jesus hath leaned for repose
   I will not, I will not desert to his foes.
   That soul, though all hell should endeavor to shake,
   I'll never, no never, no never forsake."

Immortal, Invisible, God Only Wise

Walter Chalmers Smith (1824-1908) was born in Scotland and educated in Edinburgh and Aberdeen. Ordained as a minister in the Free Church (Presbyterian), he served four different parishes–three in Scotland and one in London. In 1867 he published a collection of hymn texts–*Hymns of Christ and the Christian Life.* Among the selections was a paean of praise, "Immortal, Invisible, God Only Wise," based on I Timothy 1:17, which reads: "Now unto the King eternal, immortal, invisible, the only wise God, be honor and glory forever and ever."

The tune ST. DENIO is based on an anonymous folk melody from Wales. In 1839, a Welsh hymnal–*Caniadau y Cyssegr*–first notated the melody, with a four-part hymn-style harmonization by one John Roberts. Due to the unusual meter of "Immortal, Invisible, God Only Wise"–four lines of 11 syllables each–Smith may well have had this tune in mind as he wrote his hymn text, though his collection contained no music.

ST. DENIO
Welsh Hymn Tune, 1839

Walter Chalmers Smith, 1867

light in - ac - ces - si - ble hid from our eyes. Most

Organ: no pedal

bless - ed, most glo - rious, the An - cient of Days, Al -

Organ: resume pedal

might - y, vic - to - rious, Thy great name we praise.

(D.S.)

molto rit.

2. Unresting, unhasting, and silent as light,
   Nor wanting, nor wasting, Thou rulest in might;
   Thy justice, like mountains, high soaring above
   Thy clouds, which are fountains of goodness and love.

3. To all, life Thou givest–to both great and small;
   In all life Thou livest–the true Life of all.
   Thy wisdom so boundless, Thy mercy so free,
   Eternal Thy goodness, for naught changeth Thee.

4. Great Father of glory, pure Father of light,
   Thine angels adore Thee, all veiling their sight.
   All laud we would render–O help us to see
   'Tis only the splendor of light hideth Thee.

FJH2023

In the Cross of Christ I Glory

John Bowring was born in England in 1792. A brilliant linguist as an adult, he was said to have been fluent in 22 languages, besides having a working knowledge of many more. In addition to his prolific output of essays, original poems, and hymns, he enjoyed translating poems from other languages. Always active in British politics, he was appointed consul general for the English government in Hong Kong, China. During this period he once sailed down the Chinese coast to Macao, where the Portugese explorer Vasco da Gama had 400 years earlier built a magnificent cathedral overlooking the harbor. While the structure itself had been destroyed by a typhoon, its tower remained–topped by a great bronze cross outlined against the sky. The scene struck Bowry as symbolic of the Kingdom of God–towering above the wreckage of earthly kingdoms which have come and gone–and in a short time the text "In the Cross of Christ I Glory" came to him. He eventually became the governor of Hong Kong, a position for which he has received mixed reviews from historians. Some claim he was a benevolent official who promoted the general welfare of the Chinese. Others have accused him of leading a heavy-handed administration which may well have instigated the second Opium War in 1856. But the British crown's perception of his service (including two stints in Parliament) was positive at the time, and he was knighted late in life.

Ithamar Conkey, born of Scottish ancestry in Massachusetts in 1815, became a noted church musician and bass singer. One stormy Sunday morning in 1849, only one choir member showed up at Central Baptist Church in Norwich, Connecticut, where Conkey was serving as organist. Feeling somewhat discouraged that afternoon, he sat down at his piano to practice. His pastor was in the midst of a sermon series entitled "The Words of the Cross." As a result, Conkey had recently been exposed to Bowring's hymn text. With the exquisite poem fresh in his mind and made even more poignant by the storm that raged outside, he composed a musical setting for it. As it had long been customary to give hymn tunes names of their own, apart from their identification with particular texts, he named his new melody for the faithful soprano who alone had braved the elements that morning–Mrs. Beriah S. Rathbun.

John Bowring, 1825

RATHBUN
Ithamar Conkey, 1849

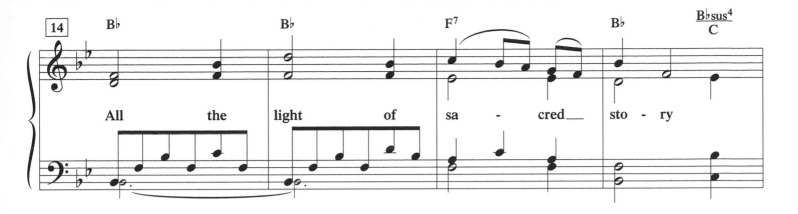

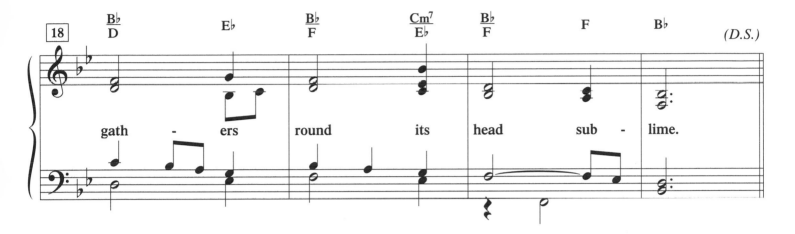

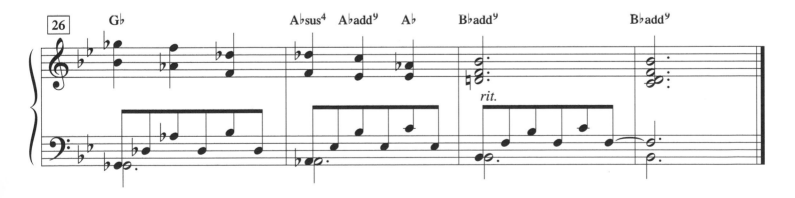

2. When the woes of life o'ertake me,
Hopes deceive, and fears annoy,
Never shall the cross forsake me.
Lo! it glows with peace and joy.

3. When the sun of bliss is beaming
Light and love upon my way,
From the cross, the radiance streaming
Adds more luster to the day.

4. Bane and blessing, pain and pleasure
By the cross are sanctified.
Peace is there that knows no measure,
Joys that through all time abide.

FJH2023

It Came Upon the Midnight Clear

Edmund Hamilton Sears (1810-1876) was born in the Massachusetts Berkshires, a direct descendant of one of the Pilgrim Fathers who had landed on Plymouth Rock in 1620. He was educated at Union College and Harvard Divinity School, becoming a Unitarian minister in 1837. In 1849, his poem "It Came Upon the Midnight Clear" appeared in the *Christian Register*, a church periodical. While at first glance it may seem ironic that a Unitarian would write what has become a favorite Christmas song, the fact is that Sears was Unitarian more by name than by conviction. This can be seen in his *Sermons and Songs of the Christian Life*, published shortly before his death, as well as in a letter to English hymnist, Bishop Bickersteth, in which Sears wrote: "Although I was educated in the Unitarian denomination, I believe and preach the divinity of Christ." A year after the poem first appeared, it was set to a tune written by Richard Storrs Willis (1819-1900), a prominent critic and editor at the *New York Tribune* who had, as a young man, studied music in Europe with Felix Mendelssohn.

CAROL

Edmund H. Sears, 1849

Richard S. Willis, 1850

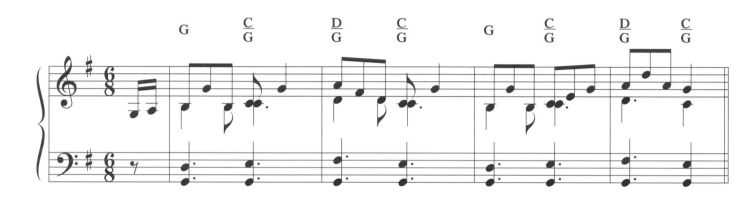

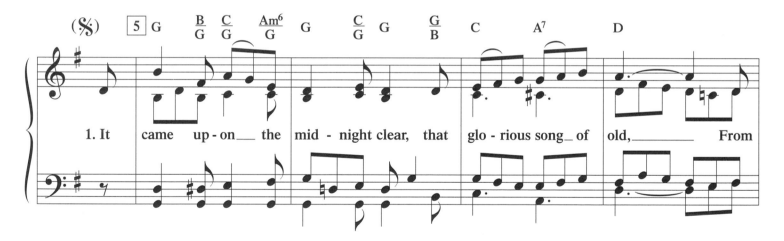

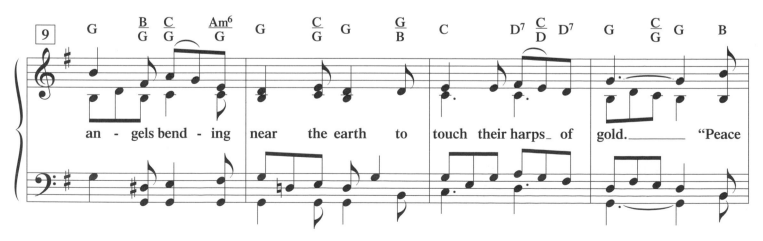

on the earth,__ good - will to men, from heav'n's_all - gra - cious King."_____ The

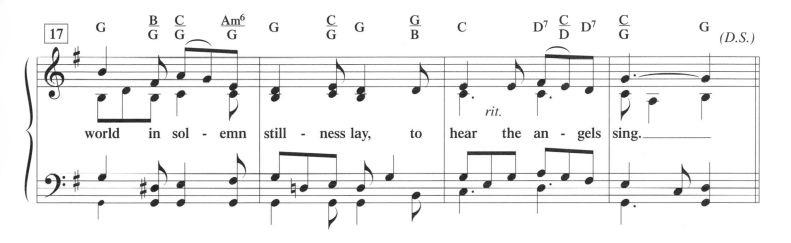

world in sol - emn still - ness lay, to hear the an - gels sing._____

(D.S.)

rit.

a tempo

rit.

2. Still through the cloven skies they come,
   With peaceful wings unfurled,
   And still their heav'nly music floats
   O'er all the weary world.
   Above its sad and lowly plains
   They bend on hov'ring wing,
   And ever o'er its Babel sounds
   The blessed angels sing.

3. Yet with the woes of sin and strife
   The world hath suffered long;
   Beneath the angel-strain have rolled
   Two thousand years of wrong.
   And man, at war with man, hears not
   The love song which they bring.
   O hush the noise, ye men of strife,
   And hear the angels sing.

4. And ye, beneath life's crushing load,
   Whose forms are bending low,
   Who toil along the climbing way
   With painful step and slow,
   Look up! for glad and golden hours
   Come swiftly on the wing.
   O rest beside the weary road
   And hear the angels sing.

5. For lo, the days are hast'ning on,
   By prophet bards foretold,
   When with the ever-circling years
   Comes round the age of gold,
   When peace shall over all the earth
   Its ancient splendors fling,
   And the whole world give back the song
   Which now the angels sing.

It Is Well with My Soul

The year was 1870, and life was good for Horatio Spafford, a successful lawyer and businessman living in Chicago with his wife Anna and their four daughters. Ever the philanthropist, he was also involved with the YMCA, McCormick Theological Seminary, and the ministry of evangelist D.L. Moody. Then came the great Chicago fire of 1871, which destroyed much of his business interests in one fell swoop. Because their home was spared, the Spaffords opened it up to many who had lost theirs. But after some time, the strain of caring for their homeless guests in addition to her own daughters took its toll on Anna's health, and Horatio decided that they all needed a vacation in Europe. But at the last minute, someone expressed an interest in buying some of his fire-damaged property. So he took his family to New York where he put them on the S.S. *Ville du Havre,* the largest passenger steamer of its day, with a promise to join them in Paris just as soon as the business transaction was complete. Tragically, in the darkness of the early morning of November 22, 1873, as it was off the coast of Newfoundland, the ship was accidently rammed broadside by the *Trimountain,* a sailing vessel, sinking in 12 minutes. Anna Spafford was one of only 22 who survived (from a passenger list of 500). All four girls perished. Originally rescued by the *Trimountain* itself, Anna was transferred to a passing vessel bound for Cardiff , Wales. For two weeks, the overcrowded, understocked ship fought North Atlantic storms before reaching land. Upon arrival, Anna sent a two-word message via cable to her husband: "saved alone." Immediately Horatio traveled to the East Coast and boarded a ship for Wales. Tracing the same route taken by the *Ville du Havre,* the captain notified Spafford as they passed over the location of the disaster. Overcome with the magnitude of his losses, yet refusing to lose faith, he retreated to his cabin where he began to pour out his feelings on paper. Three years later, the resulting poem was set to music by the well-known Philip P. Bliss who, ironically, lost his life shortly thereafter in a train crash while traveling to Chicago to assist D.L. Moody in a crusade.

VILLE DU HAVRE

Horatio G. Spafford, 1873

Philip P. Bliss, 1876

(this arrangement not recommended for organ)

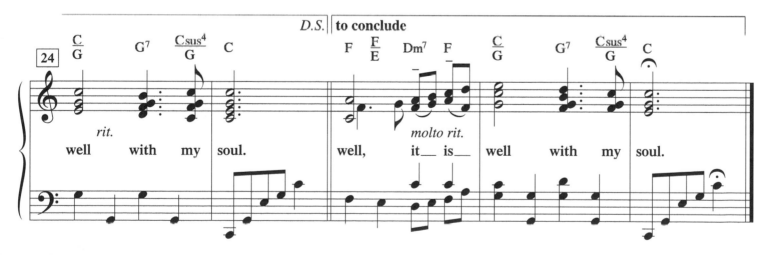

2. Though Satan should buffet, though trials should come,
   Let this blest assurance control:
   That Christ hath regarded my helpless estate
   And hath shed His own blood for my soul.

3. My sin–oh, the bliss of this glorious thought–
   My sin–not in part, but the whole–
   Is nailed to His cross, and I bear it no more!
   Praise the Lord, praise the Lord, O my soul!

4. And, Lord, haste the day when the faith shall be sight,
   The clouds be rolled back as a scroll,
   The trump shall resound and the Lord shall descend.
   Even so, it is well with my soul.

Jesus Loves Me

The prime piece of real estate known today as Constitution Island, a part of West Point Military Academy, once belonged to two sisters, Susan and Anna Warner. There they wrote books and conducted Sunday School classes for cadets from the nearby academy. Written under their respective pseudonyms–Elizabeth Wetherell and Amy Lothrop, their book *The Wide, Wide World* had become an instant best-seller, resulting in great demand for another. In 1860, they published *Say and Seal*, a thousand pages of text released in two volumes. The plot revolved around a sweet young lady named Faith Derrick, a devout Sunday School teacher, and her beau, an equally righteous young man named John Linden–also a Sunday School teacher. (Editor's note: ah, they just don't write novels like they used to!) One of their students was a lad named Johnny Fax. Volume one describes the many happy hours that the three main characters spent together, almost like a family. But in volume two, little Johnny becomes critically ill. As John cradles the dying boy in his arms, the youngster requests a song–any song. And so, in volume two of *Say and Seal*, the character John Linden begins singing, for the first time anywhere: "Jesus loves me, this I know..." A year later William B. Bradbury, well-known composer of gospel songs, set the poem to music–using a simple pentatonic scale–and added a chorus: "Yes, Jesus loves me..." And thus was born the most popular children's song of all time.

Oh, yes, the rest of the story...little Johnny died a few hours later, and the Warner sisters (no relation to the Warner brothers) later gave Constitution Island to the United States as an outright gift.

JESUS LOVES ME

Anna B. Warner, 1860

William B. Bradbury, 1861

1. Je - sus loves me! this I know, for the Bi - ble tells me so.

Lit - tle ones to Him be - long; they are weak, but He is strong.

Organ: no pedal

Organ: add pedal

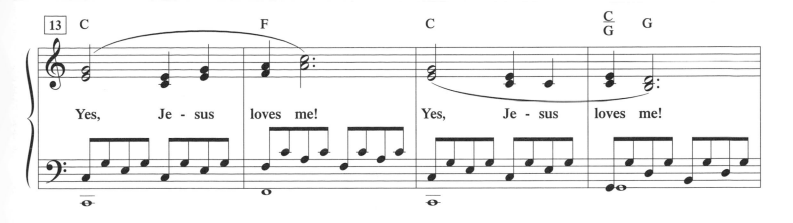

Yes, Je - sus loves me! Yes, Je - sus loves me!

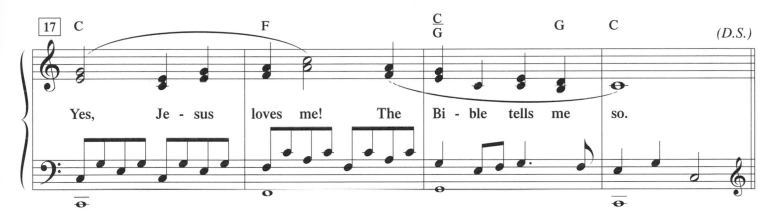

Yes, Je - sus loves me! The Bi - ble tells me so.

Delicately, like a music box

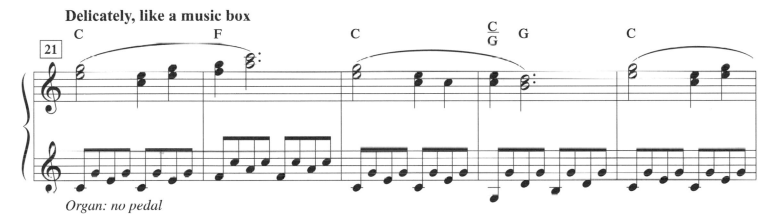

Organ: no pedal

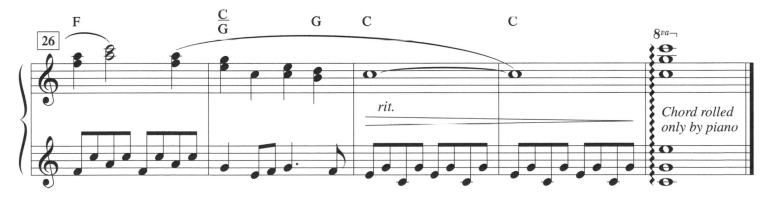

rit.

Chord rolled only by piano

Original text
(most modern hymnals contain some alternate verses)

2. Jesus loves me, He who died,
   Heaven's gate to open wide;
   He will wash away my sin,
   Let His little child come in.

3. Jesus loves me, loves me still,
   Though I'm weak and very ill;
   From His shining throne on high
   Comes to watch me where I lie.

4. Jesus loves me; He will stay
   Close beside me all the way.
   Then His little child will take
   Up to heav'n for His dear sake.

Jesus Shall Reign

In the late 17th century Reformed Church of England, the standard musical fare was the stilted psalmody of Sternhold and Hopkins, usually "lined out" by the leader and echoed by the congregation. In 1692, when the precocious 18-yr-old Isaac Watts complained so vehemently about the "scandalous doggerel," as Samuel Wesley called it, his deacon father challenged him to come up with something better. A week later, Watts' first hymn was sung in the evening service and was received very favorably. This opened the door to a lifetime of hymn writing, earning him the posthumous title, "Father of English Hymnody."

His 1719 hymnal, *The Psalms of David Imitated in the Language of the New Testament,* took all 150 of the Old Testament psalms and gave them a distinctly Christian or New Testament flavor. Several of those hymns have become classics, even included in new hymnals today–among them, "Jesus Shall Reign," based on Psalm 72.

DUKE STREET
John Hatton, 1793

Isaac Watts, 1719

1. Je - sus shall reign wher - e'er_____ the sun

Does his suc - ces - sive jour - neys run;

2. To Him shall endless prayer be made,
   And endless praises crown His head.
   His name like sweet perfume shall rise
   With ev'ry morning sacrifice.

3. People and realms of ev'ry tongue
   Dwell on His love with sweetest song,
   And infant voices shall proclaim
   Their earthly blessings on His name.

4. Let ev'ry creature rise and bring
   His grateful honors to our King;
   Angels descend with songs again,
   And earth repeat the loud "Amen!"

Jesus, the Very Thought of Thee

During the Middle Ages, the Roman Mass included no congregational singing–but only Gregorian chants sung in Latin. The "barbarian languages" used in everyday conversation were considered too crude for use in church music–or any aspect of worship, for that matter. In the 12th century (which many consider the golden age of Latin hymnody), one outstanding poem was created–"De Nomine Jesu"–from which four different English hymns were much later derived, including the one which was translated "Jesus, the Very Thought of Thee." While no definitive documentation has been found as to the authorship of the original Latin text, scholars generally attribute it to Bernard of Clairvaux, a pious French monk. Born in 1090, the son of a knight who took part in the First Crusade but didn't return, he originally planned to be a priest but later decided to enter a monastery. Three years later, at the age of 25, he founded a monastery of his own. Haggard in appearance from his extensive fasting and stoic lifestyle, he was widely known for his deep spiritual fervor and eloquent oratory. Of his pupils, thirty later became bishops, six became cardinals, and one became a pope. In 1146 he traveled through Germany and France preaching a second crusade. Of the thousands who responded to the call, only a tenth reached Palestine, and the expedition was a miserable failure. Assuming the blame, the despondent Bernard died shortly thereafter, in 1153.

Attr. to Bernard of Clairvaux, 12th century
Tr. by Edward Caswell, 1849

ST. AGNES
John B. Dykes, 1866

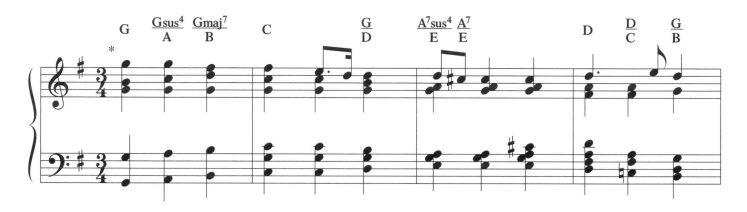

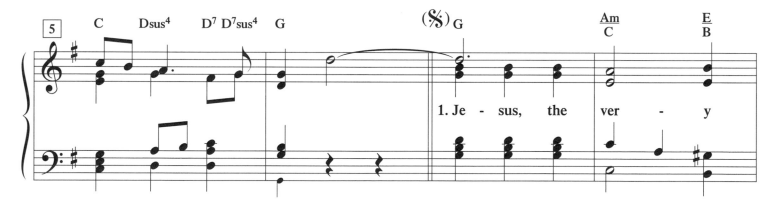

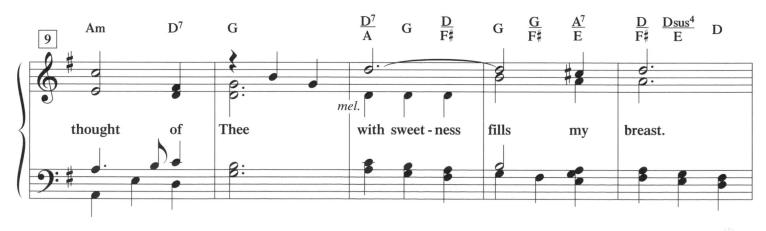

*Quoting G.F. Handel's "Largo" from *Xerxes*.

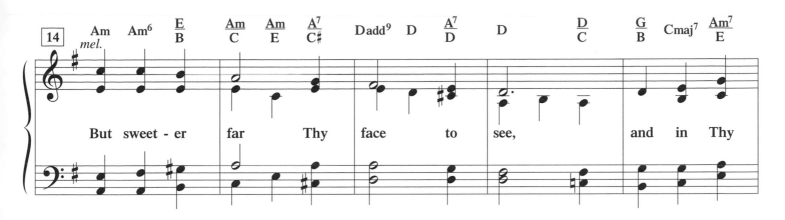

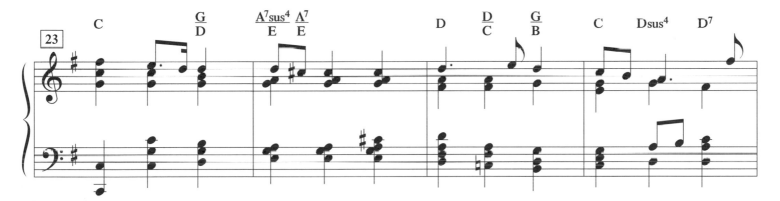

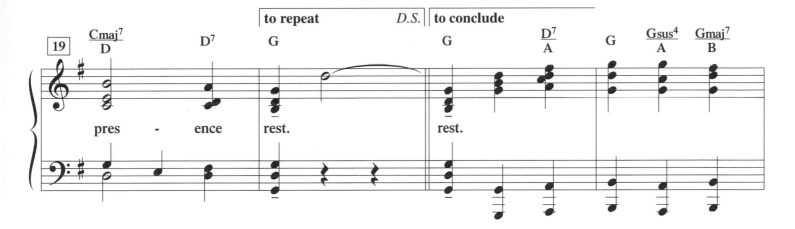

2. No voice can sing, no heart can frame,
   Nor can the mem'ry find
   A sweeter sound than Thy blest name,
   O Savior of mankind!

4. But what to those who find? Ah, this
   Nor tongue nor pen can show.
   The love of Jesus, what it is–
   None but His loved ones know.

3. O hope of ev'ry contrite heart,
   O joy of all the meek,
   To those who fall, how kind Thou art!
   How good to those who seek!

5. Jesus, our only joy be Thou,
   As Thou our prize wilt be.
   Jesus, be Thou our glory now
   And through eternity.

Joy to the World

In the late 17th century Reformed Church of England, the standard musical fare was the stilted psalmody of Sternhold and Hopkins, usually "lined out" by the leader and echoed by the congregation. In 1692, when the precocious 18-yr-old Isaac Watts complained so vehemently about the "scandalous doggerel," as Samuel Wesley called it, his deacon father challenged him to come up with something better. A week later, Watts' first hymn was sung in the evening service and was received very favorably. This opened the door to a lifetime of hymn writing, earning him the posthumous title, "Father of English Hymnody." His 1719 hymnal, *The Psalms of David Imitated in the Language of the New Testament,* took all 150 of the Old Testament psalms and gave them a distinctly Christian or New Testament flavor. Several of those hymns have become classics–among them, "Joy to the World," based on Psalm 98.

In 1741, another London-area resident–an acquaintance of Watts–George Frederick Handel, composed the monumental work, *Messiah.* At that point, neither man realized that he had provided components for what would become one of the best-loved Christmas carols of all time. It remained for the Boston choir director and composer, Lowell Mason, to combine their ideas over a century later, taking a motif from *Messiah* and continuing in Handel's highly melismatic style–creating a musical setting that was worthy of Watts' triumphant text.

Isaac Watts, 1719

ANTIOCH
G. F. Handel, 1741
Adapted by Lowell Mason, 1848

1. Joy to the world! the Lord is come; let earth re-ceive her King._____ Let ev-'ry_ heart_____ pre-pare_ Him_ room,_____ and

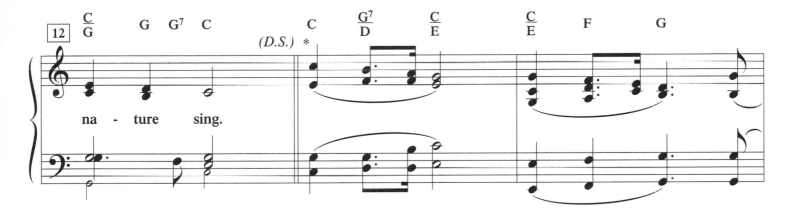

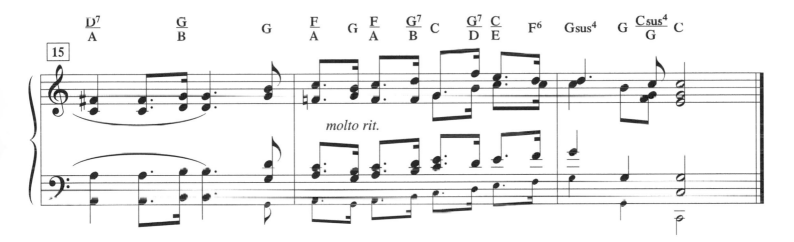

*Quoting G.F. Handel's "Lift Up Your Heads, O Ye Gates" from *Messiah*.

2. Joy to the earth! the Savior reigns;
   Let men their songs employ;
   While fields and floods, rocks, hills, and plains
   Repeat the sounding joy,
   Repeat the sounding joy,
   Repeat, repeat the sounding joy.

3. No more let sin and sorrow grow,
   Nor thorns infest the ground.
   He comes to make His blessings flow
   Far as the curse is found,
   Far as the curse is found,
   Far as, far as the curse is found.

4. He rules the world with truth and grace,
   And makes the nations prove
   The glories of His righteousness,
   And wonders of His love,
   And wonders of His love,
   And wonders, wonders of His love.

Joyful, Joyful, We Adore Thee

The hymn text, "Joyful, Joyful, We Adore Thee," was written in 1907 by Henry van Dyke (1852-1933) during a preaching visit to Williams College in Massachusetts. Rev. van Dyke presented the text to the president of the college one morning at breakfast, citing the nearby Berkshire mountains as his inspiration. It was first published in the *Presbyterian Hymnal,* 1911, where it was set to "Ode to Joy," the finale in Beethoven's *Ninth Symphony.* Educated at Princeton, van Dyke became known as one of the most outstanding preachers in America during his second pastorate, a 17-year tenure at Brick Presbyterian Church in New York City. In 1900 he was named Professor of English Literature at his alma mater. In 1913, President Woodrow Wilson appointed him to an ambassadorship in Luxemburg and the Netherlands. Four years later, as the United States became involved in World War I, he accepted a commission as a chaplain in the Navy. Other posts in his long and illustrious career: Moderator of the General Assembly of the Presbyterian Church, Commander of the Legion of Honor, and President of the National Institute of Arts and Letters. Active to the end of his life, he was serving as chairman of the Committee of Revision of the Presbyterian *Book of Common Worship* when he died at the age of 81.

Throughout his life, van Dyke wrote many fine poems and hymns. His foreword in one collection of verse rings true even today, a century later:

"These verses are simple expressions of common Christian feelings and desires in this present time, hymns of today that may
be sung together by people who know the thought of the age, and are not afraid that any truth of science will destroy religion
or that any revolution on earth will overthrow the kingdom of heaven. Therefore these are hymns of trust and joy and hope."

HYMN TO JOY
Ludwig van Beethoven, 1824

Henry van Dyke, 1907

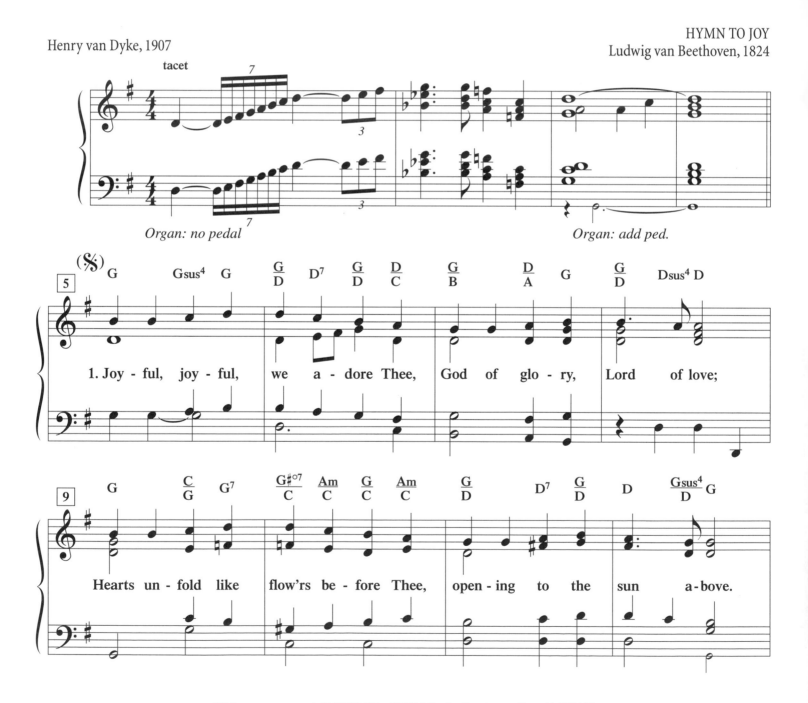

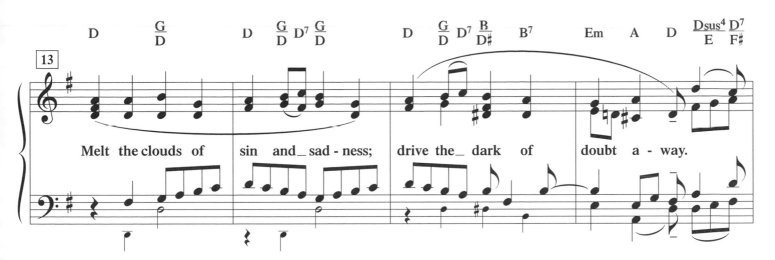

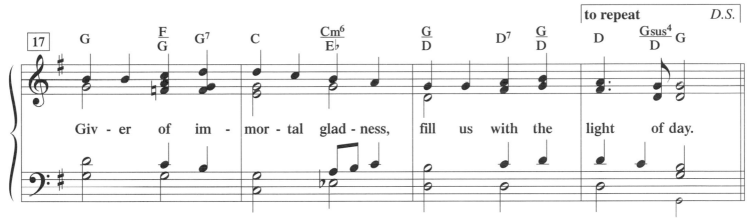

2. All Thy works with joy surround Thee;
Earth and heav'n reflect Thy rays.
Stars and angels sing around Thee,
Center of unbroken praise.
Field and forest, vale and mountain,
Flowery meadow, flashing sea,
Chanting bird and flowing fountain
Call us to rejoice in Thee.

3. Thou art giving and forgiving,
Ever blessing, ever blest,
Wellspring of the joy of living,
Ocean depth of happy rest!
Thou our Father, Christ our brother–
All who live in love are Thine.
Teach us how to love each other;
Lift us to the joy divine!

4. Mortals join the mighty chorus
Which the morning stars began.
Father-love is reigning o'er us;
Binding woman, child, and man.
Ever singing, march we onward,
Victors in the midst of strife.
Joyful music leads us sunward
In the triumph song of life.

FJH2023

Just As I Am

"Just As I Am" has become inextricably associated with the great evangelistic crusades of Billy Graham. It's no mystery why the hymn has been the invitational song of choice for Rev. Graham: it was sung the night that he himself was converted in 1937 through the ministry of Mordecai Hamm.

Its author, Charlotte Elliott, though she lived for 82 years (1789-1871), suffered debilitating illnesses all her life. Her writings reveal a constant battle against "almost overpowering weakness, languor, and exhaustion." Though fibromyalgia was not known about at that time, one has to wonder if Miss Elliott was afflicted with it or some similar autoimmune disease. Yet despite her infirmities and the resulting tendency toward depression, she was able to express her faith through a steady output of poems. On one occasion, the Genevan minister Caesar Malan (perhaps best known for his hymn tune HENDON, usually associated with the text "Take My Life, and Let It Be Consecrated") visited the Elliott home in Brighton, England. Charlotte's later writings contain a portion of the transcript of their conversation as he gave her spiritual counsel: "You have nothing of merit to bring to God. You must come just as you are, a sinner, to the Lamb of God that taketh away the sin of the world." Some time later, in 1834, as she meditated on the doctrine of salvation by grace alone, the words of the Swiss evangelist came back to her, providing the basis for a new hymn text, "Just As I Am." Initially distributed in tract form, it was soon included in a hymnal to which she contributed heavily–*The Invalid's Hymn Book, 2nd Ed.*, published in 1836.

WOODWORTH
William B. Bradbury, 1849

Charlotte Elliot, 1834

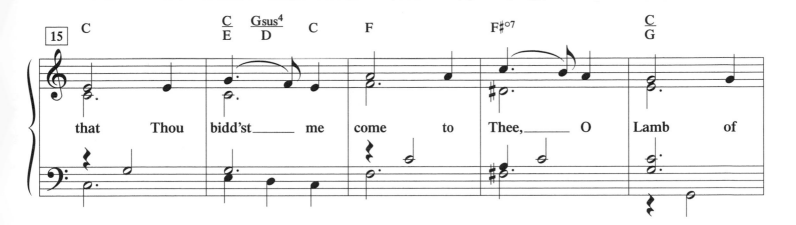

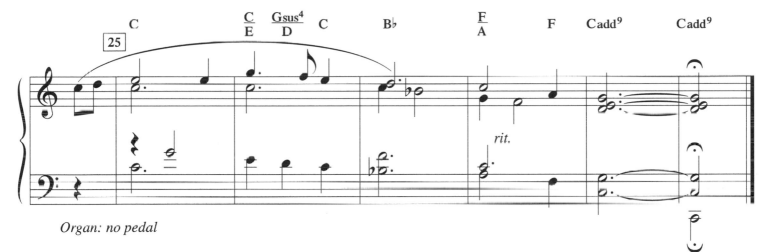

Organ: no pedal

Organ: add pedal

2. Just as I am, and waiting not
   To rid my soul of one dark blot,
   To Thee whose blood can cleanse each spot,
   O Lamb of God, I come! I come!

3. Just as I am, though tossed about
   With many a conflict, many a doubt,
   Fightings and fears within, without,
   O Lamb of God, I come! I come!

4. Just as I am–poor, wretched, blind.
   Sight, riches, healing of the mind,
   Yea, all I need, in Thee I find.
   O Lamb of God, I come! I come!

5. Just as I am, Thou wilt receive,
   Wilt welcome, pardon, cleanse, relieve.
   Because Thy promise I believe,
   O Lamb of God, I come! I come!

6. Just as I am, Thy love unknown
   Hath broken every barrier down;
   Now to be Thine, yea, Thine alone,
   O Lamb of God, I come! I come!

Lead On, O King Eternal

Henry T. Smart was born in London in 1813. Though his father prevailed on him to enter the legal profession, Henry's heart was set on a career in music and he soon dropped out of law school. With the exception of a few violin lessons, Smart trained himself in all aspects of music. At the age of 22, he composed the tune LANCASHIRE for the celebration of the 300th anniversary of The Reformation. That tune was used as the setting for many a hymn text to follow, including Reginald Heber's "From Greenland's Icy Mountains." It was certainly familiar to the student body at Andover Theological Seminary in Massachusetts in 1888 when they asked their poetically-inclined classmate, Ernest Warburton Shurtleff, to write a hymn for their graduation ceremony. Shurtleff, 26 years old at the time, had graduated from Harvard and was making quite a splash in literary circles when he enrolled at Andover to study for the ministry. The resulting text, "Lead On, O King Eternal," reflected the theme of a "social gospel" that was sweeping the United States at that time. Set to the sturdy LANCASHIRE tune written 53 years before, the hymn was a stirring march for the graduating ministerial students. Shurtleff went on to pastor three different Congregational churches in Massachusetts and Minnesota. In 1905, he organized the American Church in Frankfort, Germany. He then moved to Paris, where he ministered to college students. At the outbreak of World War I, he remained in Paris where he became vitally involved in relief work. And it was there that he died in 1917, at the age of 55. His collaborator on "Lead On, O King Eternal," Henry Smart, had gone on to write many other hymn tunes, including REGENT SQUARE ("Angels from the Realms of Glory"). When Smart died in 1879 at the age of 66, he was considered the greatest conductor in England, a feat made even more amazing by the fact that he was totally blind.

LANCASHIRE

Ernest W. Shurtleff, 1888

Henry T. Smart, 1835

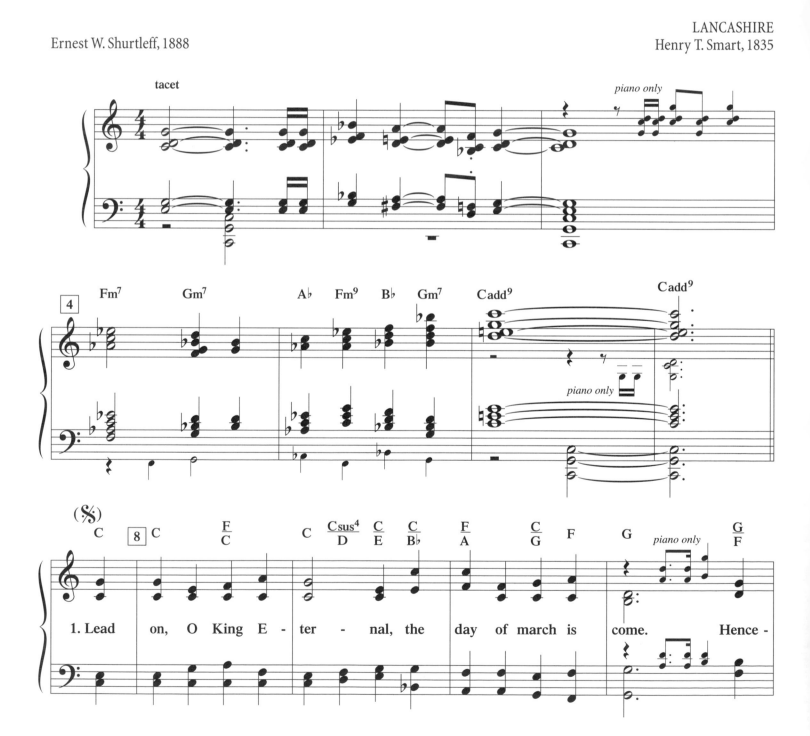

93

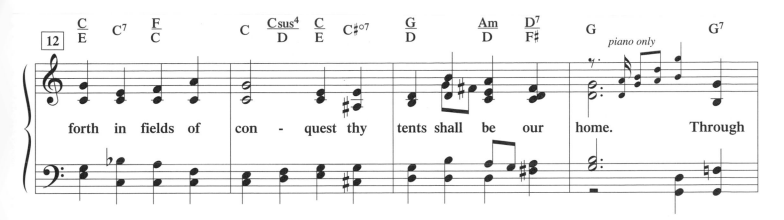

forth in fields of con - quest thy tents shall be our home. Through

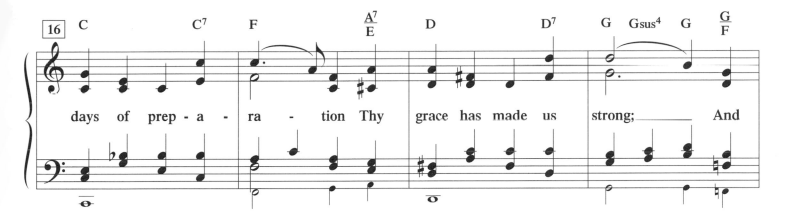

days of prep - a - ra - tion Thy grace has made us strong;_____ And

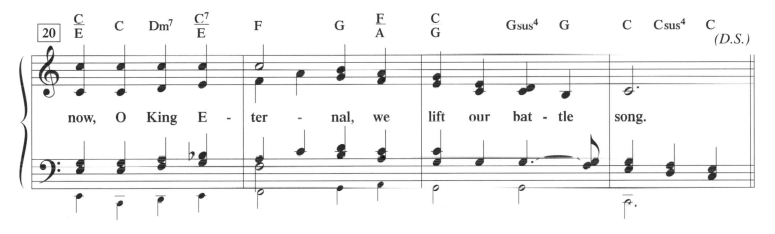

now, O King E - ter - nal, we lift our bat - tle song.

2. Lead on, O King Eternal,
   Till sin's fierce war shall cease,
   And holiness shall whisper
   The sweet amen of peace.
   For not with swords' loud clashing,
   Nor roll of stirring drums;
   With deeds of love and mercy
   The heav'nly kingdom comes.

3. Lead on, O King Eternal.
   We follow, not with fears;
   For gladness breaks like morning
   Where'er Thy face appears.
   The cross is lifted o'er us;
   We journey in its light.
   The crown awaits the conquest;
   Lead on, O God of might.

FJH2023

Let Us Break Bread Together

*The Africans who were brought to the American South on slave ships were very musical people, accustomed to expressing religious ideas in song. Sometimes they would pick up pieces of hymns or biblical text–perhaps by waiting outside the churches–and would incorporate these words and melodies into their songs. Biblical stories such as Daniel in the lions' den, the Israelites' slavery in Egypt, and the sufferings of Christ–they all spoke powerful messages of hope to those who were oppressed. Sometimes the songs were created as a way of pouring out to God their deepest prayers, desires, and frustrations.

The slaves would sing while working all day, and then would often meet at night, sometimes secretly for fear of punishment, where they would improvise in song and dance for hours, even after a hard day's work. These were songs of survival, songs that gave the courage to go on living when life seemed to be nothing but pain. They were created all throughout the 200 years of slavery, although they weren't known to most Americans until the latter half of the 19th century.

"Let Us Break Bread Together" is one of these "spirituals"–as they became known–which has taken its place in standard hymnody. Among historians, there is strong speculation that it was originally a "gathering song," used to announce an unauthorized meeting. When the traditional call–a drumbeat–was outlawed in some southern states, this song evolved as a substitute, with a probable first stanza: "let us praise God together…"

LET US BREAK BREAD
Traditional Spiritual

Traditional Spiritual

*First two paragraphs based on the foreword in Teresa Wilhelmi's FJH piano collection, *Poor Wayfaring Stranger*, FF1424.

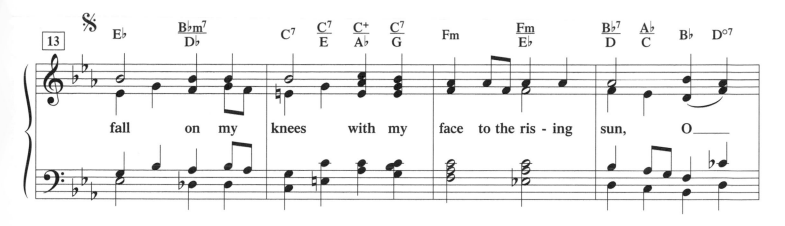

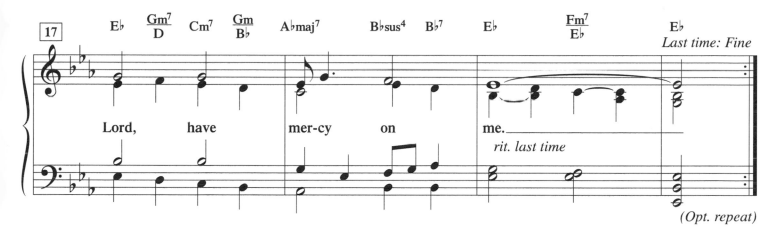

2. Let us drink the cup together on our knees.
Let us drink the cup together on our knees.
When I fall on my knees with my face to the rising sun,
O Lord, have mercy on me.

3. Let us praise God together on our knees.
Let us praise God together on our knees.
When I fall on my knees with my face to the rising sun,
O Lord, have mercy on me.

My Country, 'Tis of Thee

Shortly after the end of the Napoleonic Wars, when "the little corporal" was defeated, the German poet Siegfrid A. Mahlmann composed a patriotic hymn of supplication for Saxony–"Gott Segne Sachsenland." When first performed in 1815, it was sung to an anonymous tune which had first appeared in a 1744 collection, *Thesaurus Musicus*. In 1831, an American educator–William C. Woodbridge–collected a number of songs, including this one, while studying European school systems. Upon returning to Boston, he gave all the music to famed composer and hymnal compiler Lowell Mason, thinking that Mason might find some of it useful in future publications. But because the texts were in German, which Mason was unable to translate, he wanted someone else to sift through the material to see if any was worthy of further consideration. He remembered a brilliant student at Boston's Andover Seminary–Samuel Francis Smith. Twenty-four years old at the time, Smith was a Harvard graduate with a working knowledge of 15 languages. Years later, as he recounted how "My Country, 'Tis of Thee" came into being in February of 1832, Smith recalled leafing through one of the books when his eye rested on the tune which is now known as AMERICA. He liked the "spirited movement" of it, not realizing at the time that the tune had also come to be used in Great Britain for "God Save the King." Glancing at the German words he saw that they were patriotic, and immediately felt compelled to write a patriotic hymn of his own. Picking up a scrap of paper lying nearby, he wrote the new text in half an hour. The following July 4, Mason's children's choir premiered the song in a Boston park, and the rest is history. (Incidentally, two years later, in 1834, a New England minister–Charles T. Brooks–translated the original German poem into English, and revisions were made soon thereafter by another minister–John S. Dwight. The resulting hymn, "God Bless Our Native Land," also sung to the tune AMERICA, is somewhat more devotional than "My Country, 'Tis of Thee" and would be a valid option in many settings where a prayer for one's country is desired.)

During his lifetime, Samuel F. Smith pastored several large churches, wrote numerous books, was a language professor, held important posts in his denomination (Baptist), and authored some 150 additional hymns–the most famous of which is the great call to missionary service, "The Morning Light Is Breaking," also written in 1832. Active to the end, he continued preaching, writing, and learning. In fact, in his 86th year, he was found to be searching for a textbook that would allow him to learn the Russian language! Finally, in 1895, at the age of 87, he died at a train station while on route to a preaching engagement at a neighboring town.

Samuel F. Smith, 1832

AMERICA
Anonymous, ca. 1744

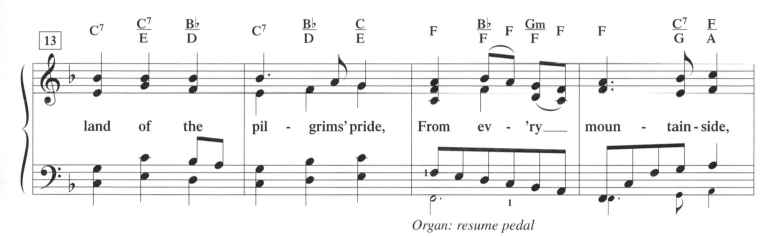

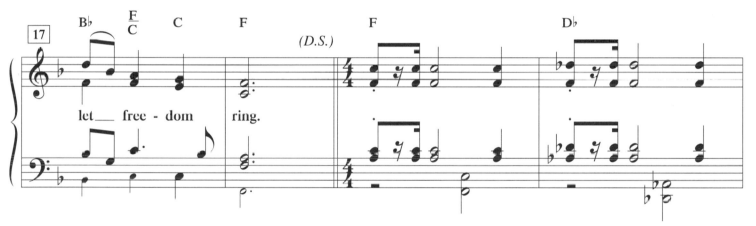

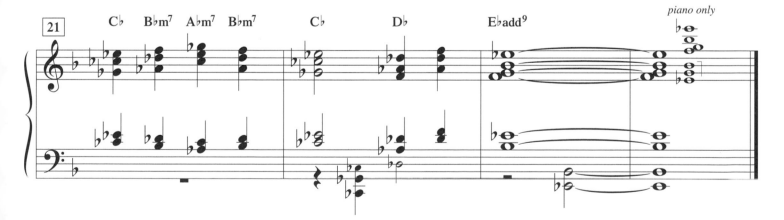

2. My native country, Thee,
   Land of the noble free,
   Thy name I love.
   I love Thy rocks and rills,
   Thy woods and templed hills;
   My heart with rapture thrills
   Like that above.

3. Let music swell the breeze,
   And ring from all the trees
   Sweet freedom's song.
   Let mortal tongues awake;
   Let all that breathe partake;
   Let rocks their silence break–
   The sound prolong.

4. Our fathers' God, to Thee,
   Author of liberty,
   To Thee we sing:
   Long may our land be bright
   With freedom's holy light;
   Protect us by Thy might,
   Great God, our King!

My Faith Looks Up to Thee

Ray Palmer, a direct descendant of John and Priscilla Alden, was born in Rhode Island in 1808. His family's poverty forced him to quit school at the age of 13 to seek employment. Working in a Boston dry goods store, the teenaged Palmer was unusually devout for his age, despite the misfortune of having to miss out on a formal education. His pastor, however, recognized the innate intelligence of the lad and helped find a way for him to resume his schooling. Eventually graduating from Phillips Andover Academy, then Yale University, Palmer became a teacher in a girls' school located in New York City while pursuing further graduate studies in preparation for the ministry. One evening, the exhausted 22-year-old was reading a short German poem which portrayed a penitent sinner kneeling before the Cross. After translating the the two-verse poem, Palmer was inspired to continue with four stanzas of his own, penciling them into his spiritual journal. Four years later, while walking down a busy street back in Boston, Palmer happened to meet Lowell Mason, a famous composer who had recently moved from Savannah, Georgia. In the course of their conversation, Mason mentioned that he was compiling material for a new hymnbook, *Spiritual Songs for Social Worship*, and wondered if Palmer had written anything that he could consider. Remembering the poem in his pocket notebook, Palmer showed "My Faith Looks Up to Thee" to Mason. The latter immediately recognized its potential as a hymn and stepped into a nearby store where he could write out a copy. That night Mason wrote the tune OLIVET as a vehicle for the text, and the two have been inextricably linked ever since. The next year, 1835, Palmer was ordained as a Congregational minister. After serving for a total of 30 years in two pastorates, he was elected corresponding secretary of the American Congregational Union–a position he held for 13 years until failing health forced him to retire. In his lifetime, he is known to have written 38 original hymns in addition to translating many Latin hymns for use in America–the most famous of which is Bernard of Clairvaux's "Jesus, Thou Joy of Loving Hearts." His whole life was characterized by an unusually strong devotion to Christ. Shortly before his death in 1887, he was heard quoting the last stanza of one of his lesser-known hymns, "Jesus, These Eyes Have Never Seen":

When death these mortal eyes shall seal,
And still this throbbing heart,
The rending veil shall Thee reveal,
All glorious as Thou art.

OLIVET
Lowell Mason, 1834

Ray Palmer, 1830

2. May Thy rich grace impart
Strength to my fainting heart,
My zeal inspire.
As Thou hast died for me,
Oh, may my love for Thee
Pure, warm, and changeless be,
A living fire.

3. While life's dark maze I tread,
And griefs around me spread,
Be Thou my Guide.
Bid darkness turn to day;
Wipe sorrow's tears away;
Nor let me ever stray
From Thee aside!

4. When ends life's transient dream,
When death's cold, sullen stream
Shall o'er me roll,
Blest Savior, then in love
Fear and distrust remove.
O bear me safe above–
A ransomed soul.

Now Thank We All Our God

Martin Rinkart was born in Eilenburg, Saxony (now Germany) in 1586, the son of a cooper. He was educated first at a Latin school and then at the University of Leipzig. After holding various pastoral offices in small towns, in 1617 he was appointed the archdeacon of the Lutheran church in his home town. The next year, 1618, the bloody conflict which would later be known as the Thirty Years' War began. Because Eilenburg was a walled city, it became a shelter for thousands of refugees–civilians as well as political and military fugitives. In 1636, in the midst of the turmoil, Rinkart published a small volume entitled *Jesu Hertz-Buchlein,* in which appeared "Tisch-Gebetlein"–or, a short grace before meals. Believed to have been written for his children, its first two stanzas are based on the Apocryphal book *Ecclesiasticus* 50:29-32, and the third stanza is based on the ancient doxology, "Gloria Patri." Eleven years later, in 1647, Johann Crüger published an important collection, *Praxis Pictatis Melica,* in which he gave Rinkart's text the tune known as NUN DANKET. Almost two centuries later, in 1840, Felix Mendelssohn harmonized the tune as it appears in hymnals today. And though it has been translated many times, it's the 1858 Catherine Winkworth version known as "Now Thank We All Our God" which has gained popular acceptance.

In 1637, the year after this hymn was written, the overcrowding and lack of sufficient food and sanitation finally overwhelmed Eilenburg, and a great plague hit, decimating the population. Of the 8,000 who died in that one city alone, including his wife and the only other two pastors in the city, Rinkart conducted approximately 4,500 of the funerals–sometimes holding 40-50 services a day. On one occasion the Swedish army attacked the town, driving out the forces who had sought refuge within. Their general, enraged because the city had not welcomed him, ordered the pestilence-stricken residents to pay a tribute of 30,000 thaler ($25,000). Knowing how destitute his people were, Rinkart led a large group out to the army encampment to plead their cause. When his initial entreaty was rebuffed, the pastor is quoted as saying, "Come, my children, we can find no mercy with men; let us take refuge with God." They then fell to their knees in fervent prayer, after which they sang a popular hymn of the day, "When in the Hour of Utmost Need." Like the unjust judge in Jesus' parable, the commander relented under the impassioned and prolonged plea, reducing his demand to 1,350 thaler. Even that sum was more than the city could readily pay, but Rinkart mortgaged his future in order to pay his share and still be able to provide food for his family. When the Peace of Westphalia was signed in 1648, thus ending the war, the Elector of Saxony ordered that Thanksgiving services be held in every church. He even designated the text from which the ministers were to preach–the same passage from *Ecclesiasticus* on which Rinkart's hymn was based. Unfortunately, the good pastor was unable to long enjoy the peacetime; the strain of a 30-year wartime ministry had taken its toll, and the worn and broken man died one year later, in 1649.

Johann Crüger (1598-1662) was born in Niederlausitz, Prussia (now northern Germany). After studying music and theology, in 1622 he was named organist at the Nikolaikirche (St. Nikolai Church) in Berlin. A close colleague of the hymnist Paul Gerhardt, he composed melodies for many of Gerhardt's texts. In addition Crüger composed sacred choral and instrumental works, and also wrote extensively on the theory and practice of music in general. His most enduring hymn tunes include HERZLIEBSTER JESU; JESU, MEINE FREUDE; and NUN DANKET.

Martin Rinkart, 1636
Tr. by Catherine Winkworth, 1858

NUN DANKET
Johann Crüger, 1647

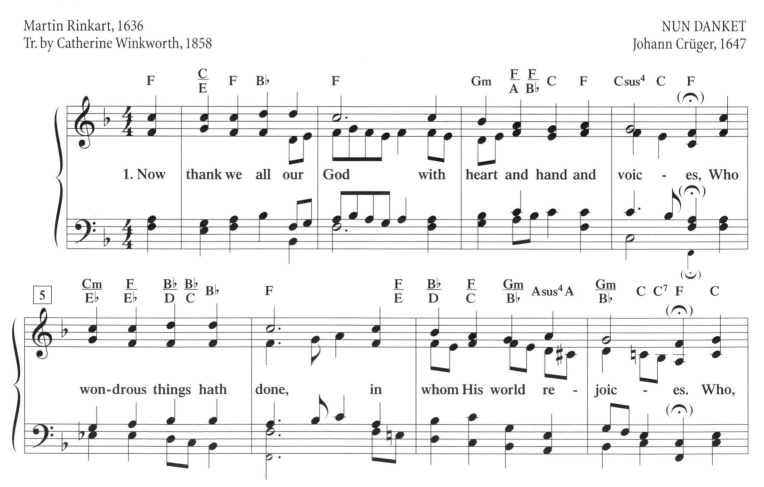

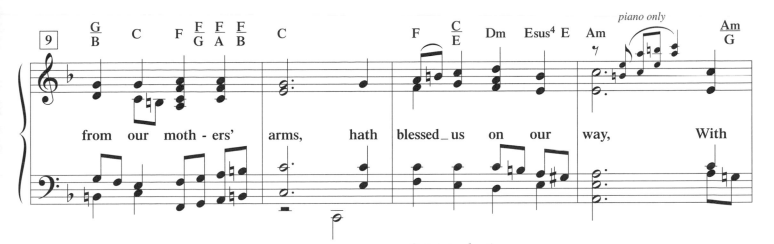

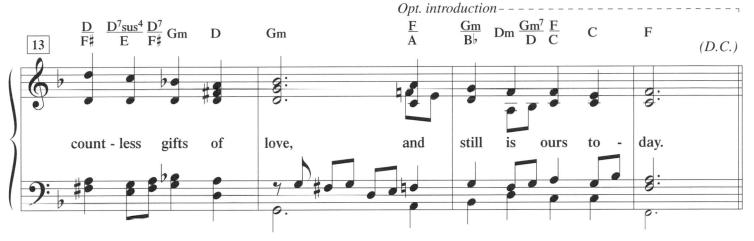

2. Oh, may this bounteous God
   Through all our life be near us,
   With ever joyful hearts
   And blessed peace to cheer us;
   And keep us in His grace,
   And guide us when perplexed,
   And free us from all ills
   In this world and the next.

3. All praise and thanks to God
   The Father now be given,
   The Son, and Him who reigns
   With them in highest heaven,
   The one eternal God,
   Whom earth and heav'n adore;
   For thus it was, is now,
   And shall be evermore.

FJH2023

O Come, All Ye Faithful

Both the text and the tune of "O Come, All Ye Faithful" are attributed to John F. Wade (1711-1786), who is thought to have written this Latin carol around 1743. Living and working in the great Catholic Center at Douay, France, Wade was a layman who copied music and taught church music and Latin.

In 1841, Frederick Oakeley (1802-1880), a minister in the Church of England, provided the English translation which is commonly used today. Later, Oakeley became interested in the Oxford Movement and converted to Catholicism, becoming a canon of Westminster in 1852.

Latin Hymn: Attr. to John F. Wade, ca. 1743
Tr. by Frederick Oakeley, 1841

ADESTE FIDELES
Attr. to John F. Wade, ca. 1743

2. Sing, choirs of angels; sing in exultation.
   O sing, all ye bright hosts of heav'n above.
   Glory to God, all glory in the highest!

   O come, let us adore Him!
   O come, let us adore Him!
   O come, let us adore Him, Christ, the Lord!

3. Yea, Lord, we greet Thee, born this happy morning.
   O Jesus, to Thee be all glory giv'n:
   Word of the Father, now in flesh appearing!

   O come, let us adore Him!
   O come, let us adore Him!
   O come, let us adore Him–Christ, the Lord!

O Come, O Come, Emmanuel

The origin of "O Come, O Come, Emmanuel" is cloaked in obscurity, with sources listing its beginnings anywhere from the seventh century to the twelfth. The text is based on a series of seven antiphons traditionally sung on successive days in Advent vesper services leading up to the Christ Mass, a celebration which later became known as Christmas. Each antiphon greeted the anticipated Savior by one of the many titles given Him in Scripture, such as "Emmanuel," "Rod of Jesse," "Dayspring," "Key of David," etc.

John Mason Neale (1818-1866) was a minister in the Church of England. Caught up in the Oxford Movement, he became interested in the original languages–specifically, Greek and Latin–that had cradled the early liturgies of the Church. He became a renowned translator of ancient hymns–among them, "Good Christian Men, Rejoice," "All Glory, Laud, and Honor," "Of the Father's Love Begotten," and "O Come, O Come, Emmanuel." After translating the Latin text "Veni Emmanuel" in 1851, he added the refrain that we know today. In 1854, Thomas Helmore took fragments of Gregorian chant and constructed a melody in the minor mode–an appropriate setting for the plaintive yearning for a Messiah. Today, some hymnals contain portions of a 1916 translation by Henry Sloan Coffin. Of the stanzas listed below, 1-4 are Neale's; 5-6 are Coffin's.

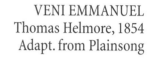

VENI EMMANUEL
Thomas Helmore, 1854
Adapt. from Plainsong

Latin Hymn
Tr. by John M. Neale, Henry S. Coffin, and others

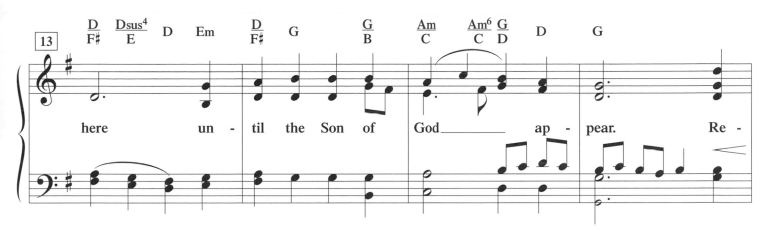

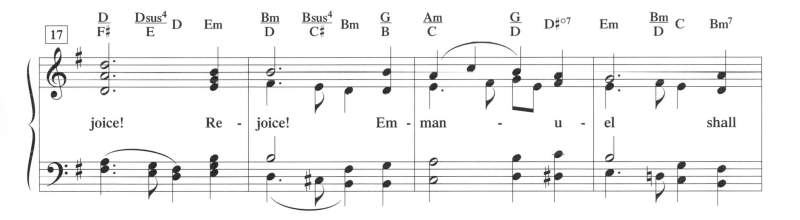

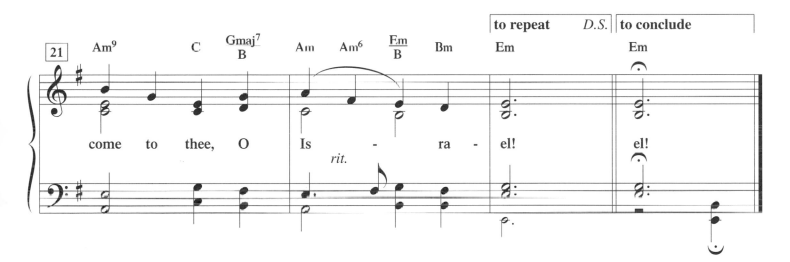

2. O come, Thou Rod of Jesse, free
   Thine own from Satan's tyranny;
   From depths of hell Thy people save
   And give them vict'ry o'er the grave.
   Rejoice...

3. O come, Thou Dayspring, come and cheer
   Our spirits by Thine advent here.
   Disperse the gloomy clouds of night,
   And death's dark shadows put to flight.
   Rejoice...

4. O come, Thou Key of David, come,
   And open wide our heav'nly home.
   Make safe the way that leads on high,
   And close the path to misery.
   Rejoice...

5. O come, Thou Wisdom from on high,
   And order all things far and nigh.
   To us the path of knowledge show,
   And cause us in her ways to go.
   Rejoice...

6. O come, Desire of nations; bind
   All peoples in one heart and mind.
   Bid envy, strife, and quarrels cease;
   Fill the whole world with heaven's peace.
   Rejoice...

O God, Our Help in Ages Past

In the late 17th century Reformed Church of England, the standard musical fare was the stilted psalmody of Sternhold and Hopkins, usually "lined out" by the leader and echoed by the congregation. In 1692, when the precocious 18-yr-old Isaac Watts complained so vehemently about the "scandalous doggerel," as Samuel Wesley called it, his deacon father challenged him to come up with something better. A week later, Watts' first hymn was sung in the evening service and was received very favorably. This opened the door to a lifetime of hymn writing, earning him the posthumous title, "Father of English Hymnody."

In 1714, England was experiencing great anxiety as the reign of their beloved Queen Anne was nearing an end. Because she had no surviving family members, speculation regarding her successor ran rampant. Watts, who was in the midst of compiling a book of hymns based on the Psalms, wrote "O God, Our Help in Ages Past," a paraphrase of Psalm 90, reminding Christians of the transitory nature of human life and history when contrasted against the timelessness of God and His reign. Distributed throughout England in leaflet form, the hymn helped to calm a nation's fears. (Eventually, in what is one of the great ironies of British history, the throne went to Anne's cousin, George of Hanover, a German who didn't even speak English!) In 1719 Watts completed the hymnbook, entitled *The Psalms of David Imitated in the Language of the New Testament,* in which he took all 150 of the Old Testament psalms and gave them a distinctly Christian or New Testament flavor. "O God, Our Help in Ages Past" was set to a sturdy, majestic tune written 11 years earlier by William Croft, organist of Westminster Abbey.

ST. ANNE
William Croft, 1708

Isaac Watts, 1719

2. Under the shadow of Thy throne
Still may we dwell secure;
Sufficient is Thine arm alone,
And our defense is sure.

3. Before the hills in order stood,
Or earth received her frame,
From everlasting Thou art God,
To endless years the same.

4. A thousand ages in Thy sight
Are like an evening gone,
Short as the watch that ends the night
Before the rising sun.

5. Time, like an ever-rolling stream,
Bears all its sons away;
They fly, forgotten, as a dream
Dies at the opening day.

FJH2023

O Little Town of Bethlehem

Phillips Brooks (1835-1893) was one of the most gifted preachers of his time. Brought up in a pious New England home, he and his siblings were required to memorize a hymn every Sunday. During the evening devotions conducted by his father, the children recited their hymns. By the time Phillips left for college, he was able to quote some two hundred hymns by memory. This treasury of verse proved to be priceless later, as Brooks frequently made effective use of hymn excerpts during his sermons. "O Little Town of Bethlehem" was written for a Sunday School Christmas festival in 1868 at the Holy Trinity Episcopal Church in Philadelphia, where Brooks was serving as rector at the time. Three years earlier, it had been his privilege to visit the Holy Land, a life-changing trip which included the opportunity to gaze on Bethlehem from the nearby hills on Christmas Eve. The beauty and wonder of that evening were still fresh in his mind when he was asked to write a new Christmas hymn. The tune was written a few days later by Lewis Redner (1831-1908), who during the week was a successful real estate broker, and on Sunday was organist and Sunday School superintendent at Holy Trinity.

ST. LOUIS
Lewis H. Redner, 1868

Phillips Brooks, 1868

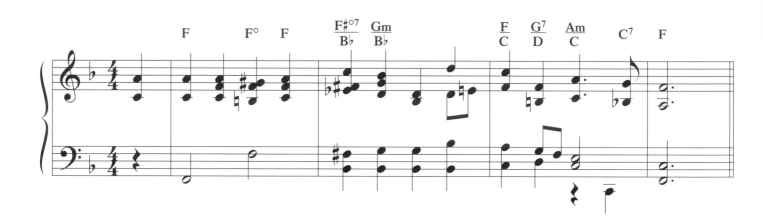

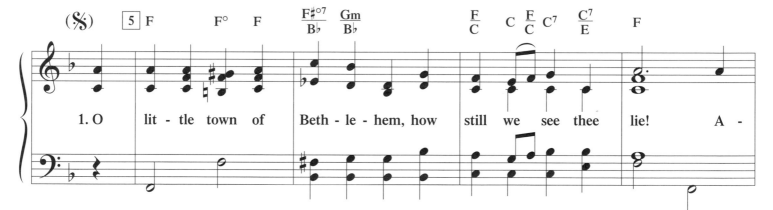

1. O lit - tle town of Beth - le - hem, how still we see thee lie! A -

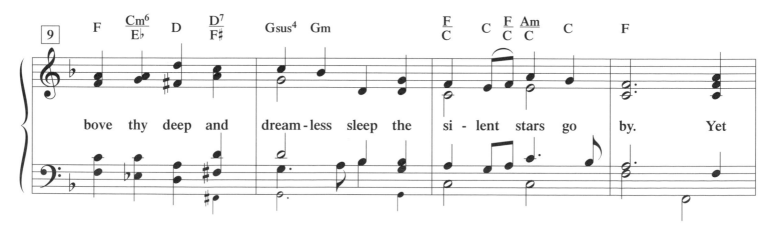

bove thy deep and dream-less sleep the si - lent stars go by. Yet

109

2. For Christ is born of Mary,
And gathered all above,
While mortals sleep, the angels keep
Their watch of wond'ring love.
O morning stars together
Proclaim the holy birth;
And praises sing to God the King,
And peace to men on earth.

3. How silently, how silently
The wondrous Gift is giv'n!
So God imparts to human hearts
The blessings of His heav'n.
No ear may hear His coming,
But in this world of sin,
Where meek souls will receive Him still,
The dear Christ enters in.

4. O holy Child of Bethlehem,
Descend on us, we pray.
Cast out our sin, and enter in;
Be born in us today.
We hear the Christmas angels
The great glad tidings tell.
O come to us; abide with us,
Our Lord, Emmanuel.

FJH2023

O Love That Wilt Not Let Me Go

George Matheson was born in Glasgow, Scotland in 1842, the son of a wealthy merchant. A brilliant scholar though partially blind, he entered Glasgow University at the age of 15. By the time he graduated with honors four years later, he was completely blind. Having felt a call to the ministry while in college, he remained at the same school for another four years of graduate studies in theology. His sister, who had learned Greek, Latin, and Hebrew in order to assist him in his ministerial preparation, remained his assistant and guide throughout his entire life. After a three-year internship at a church in Glasgow, he was given his first assignment in 1868–at Innellan, an idyllic coastal resort town. One summer evening in 1882, he composed the text "O Love That Wilt Not Let Me Go." In his own words: "It was composed with extreme rapidity; it seemed to me that its construction occupied only a few minutes, and I felt myself rather in the position of one who was being dictated to than an original artist. I was suffering from extreme mental distress, and the hymn was the fruit of pain." Though Matheson never specified the reason for his inner turmoil, the opening line of the hymn have led many to conjecture that a woman with whom he was in love had decided that she couldn't marry him because of his blindness. Many phrases in the poem hint at his affliction, e.g., "flickering torch," "borrowed ray," etc. Matheson did say that it was written on the day of his beloved sister's wedding, so that event probably exacerbated the feeling of rejection that gnawed at him. It so happened that a new collection, the *Scottish Hymnal*, was being compiled at the time. The editors became aware of Matheson's text and asked one Albert Peace to set it to music. And so, out of great pain came a beautiful hymn that took Scotland by storm and has been a comfort to millions since. Despite his physical limitations and the disappointment of love lost, Matheson enjoyed a fruitful ministry and was much appreciated by his parishioners. After 18 years at Innellan, he was called to pastor St. Bernard Church in Edinburgh, where he again attracted large congregations through his preaching, and where he remained for 13 years. In retirement he threw himself into literary efforts, authoring several volumes of prose including a devotional book, *Moments on the Mount*. Another hymn for which he is remembered is "Make Me a Captive, Lord." In the last days before his death in 1906, he was buoyed up by his own immortal words: "...the promise is not vain that morn shall tearless be."

ST. MARGARET
Albert L. Peace, 1884

George Matheson, 1882

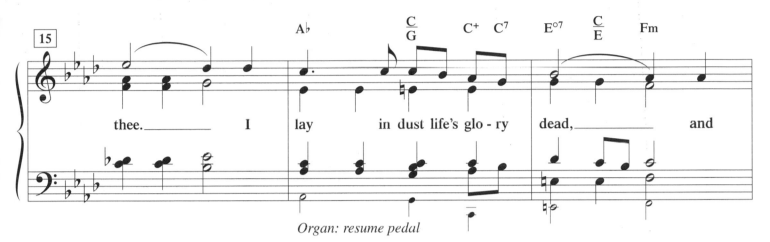

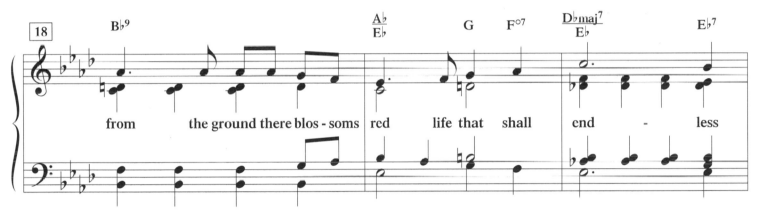

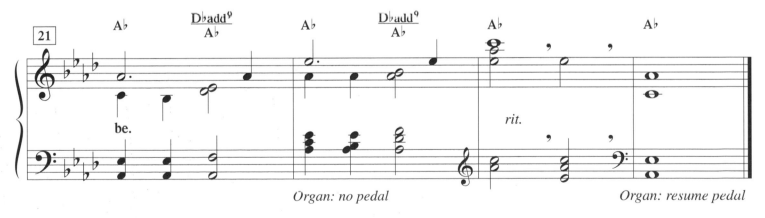

2. O Light that follow'st all my way,
I yield my flick'ring torch to Thee.
My heart restores its borrowed ray,
That in Thy sunshine's blaze its day
May brighter, fairer be.

3. O Joy that seekest me through pain,
I cannot close my heart to Thee.
I trace the rainbow through the rain,
And feel the promise is not vain
That morn shall tearless be.

O Master, Let Me Walk with Thee

Washington Gladden was born in Pennsylvania in 1836. After graduating from Williams College in 1859, he served as a minister in the Congregational Church for 55 years, the last 32 of which were spent in Columbus, Ohio. Known nationwide as one of the most distinguished clergymen of his day, Gladden was recognized for both his oratorical and writing skills. But despite his prolific output of books and magazine articles, all of which are now forgotten about, it is one little poem that has preserved his name for posterity. As an editor for the *Sunday Afternoon*, a weekly periodical, he included "O Master, Let Me Walk with Thee" in an 1879 issue. As one who was concerned about not only the spiritual and moral condition of the masses, but also campaigned for the improvement of their social and economic welfare, Gladden had often found himself the object of controversy. This poem seems to have been written with his critics in mind, especially two of the original stanzas which have subsequently been deemed dispensable by hymnal editors:

O Master, let me walk with Thee   *The sore distrust of souls sincere*
Before the taunting Pharisee;   *Who cannot read Thy judgments clear,*
Help me to bear the sting of spite,   *The dullness of the multitude,*
The hate of men who hide Thy light,   *Who dimly guess that Thou art good.*

To the end, Gladden remained hopeful that good would eventually overcome evil. In one of his last sermons, he said, "I have never doubted that the Kingdom I have always prayed for is coming; that the Gospel I have preached is true. I believe...that the nation is being saved."

MARYTON
Washington Gladden, 1879   H. Percy Smith, 1874

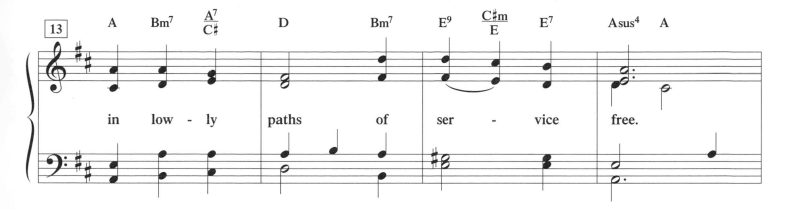

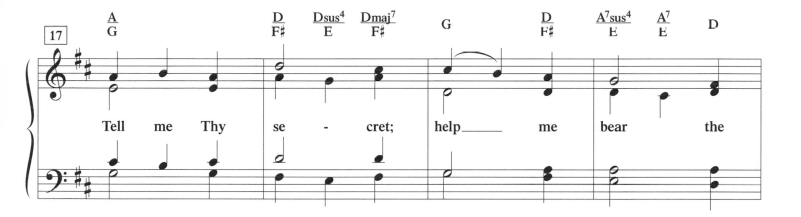

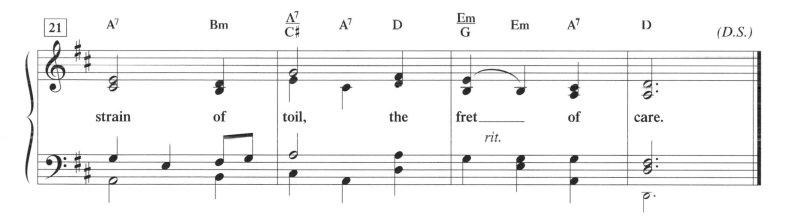

2. Help me the slow of heart to move
   By some clear, winning word of love.
   Teach me the wayward feet to stay,
   And guide them in the homeward way.

3. Teach me Thy patience! still with Thee
   In closer, dearer company,
   In work that keeps faith sweet and strong,
   In trust that triumphs over wrong.

4. In hope that sends a shining ray
   Far down the future's broad'ning way,
   In peace that only Thou canst give,
   With Thee, O Master, let me live.

O Sacred Head, Now Wounded

During the Middle Ages, the Roman Mass included no congregational singing–but only Gregorian chants sung in Latin. The "barbarian languages" used in everyday conversation were considered too crude for use in church music–or any aspect of worship, for that matter. In the 12th century (which many consider the golden age of Latin hymnody), several outstanding Latin hymns were created, including the one which after two translations is known as "O Sacred Head, Now Wounded." This extensive poem, "Salve Caput Cruentatum," originally discussed all of the places where Christ was wounded–feet, hands, side, heart, face, head, etc. While no definitive documentation has been found as to its authorship, scholars generally attribute it to Bernard of Clairvaux, a pious French monk born in 1090. The son of a knight, he originally planned to be a priest but later decided to enter a monastery. Three years later, at the age of 25, he founded a monastery of his own. Haggard in appearance from his extensive fasting and stoic lifestyle, he was widely known for his deep spiritual fervor and eloquent oratory. Of his pupils, thirty later became bishops, six became cardinals, and one became a pope. In 1146 he traveled through Germany and France preaching a second crusade. Of the thousands who responded to the call, only a tenth reached Palestine, and the expedition was a miserable failure. Assuming the blame, the despondent Bernard died shortly thereafter, in 1153.

In 1656, his poem was translated into German by Paul Gerhardt, a Lutheran pastor from Berlin. In 1729, J.S. Bach took the German translation and combined it with a hymn tune which, in 1601, had been derived from a German folksong by Hans Leo Hassler–harmonizing and arranging the tune into the chorale as we know it today. In 1830, the German text was translated into English by Dr. James Waddell Alexander, a Presbyterian minister and Professor of Ecclesiastical History at Princeton University, at which time a fourth stanza was added. Speaking of "O Sacred Head, Now Wounded," one Philip Schaff has written: "This classic hymn has shown in three tongues–Latin, German, and English–and in three confessions–Roman, Lutheran, and Reformed–with equal effect the dying love of our Savior and our boundless indebtedness to Him."

Latin Poem
Attr. to Bernard of Clairvaux, 12th century

PASSION CHORALE
Hans Leo Hassler, 1601

*Quoting John Stainer's "God So Loved the World."

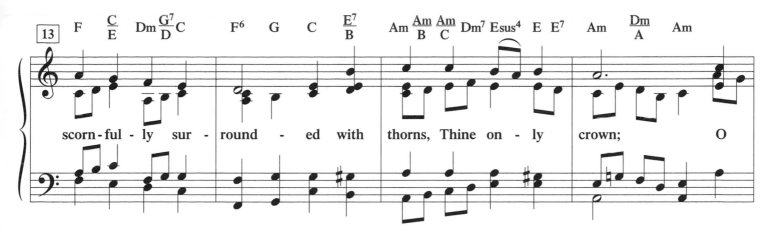

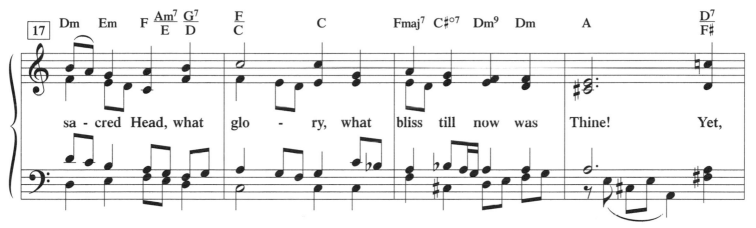

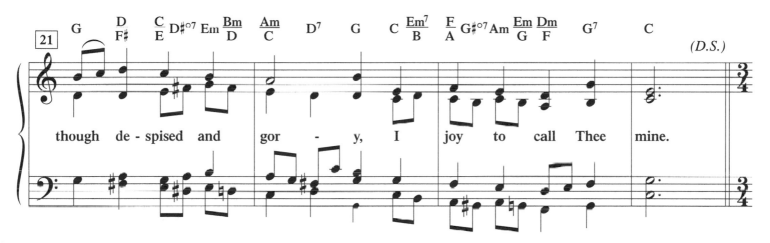

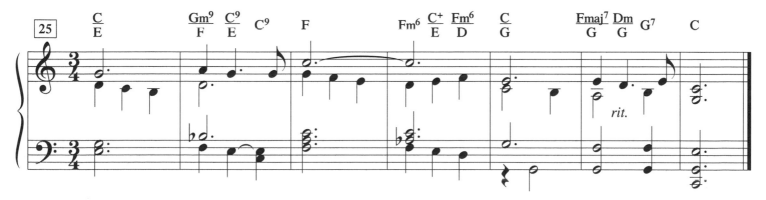

2. What Thou, my Lord, hast suffered
   Was all for sinners' gain.
   Mine, mine was the transgression,
   But Thine the deadly pain.
   Lo, here I fall, my Savior!
   'Tis I deserve Thy place.
   Look on me with Thy favor,
   And grant to me Thy grace.

3. What language shall I borrow
   To thank Thee, dearest Friend.
   For this Thy dying sorrow,
   Thy pity without end?
   O make me Thine forever;
   And, should I fainting be,
   Lord, let me never, never
   Outlive my love to Thee.

4. Be near when I am dying;
   O show Thy cross to me,
   And, for my comfort flying,
   Come, Lord, to set me free.
   These eyes, new faith receiving,
   From Thee shall never move;
   For He who dies believing
   Dies safely in Thy love.

O Worship the King

In 1785, Robert Grant was born into a wealthy and influential family in Scotland. His father, a director of the East India Company, was also a member of the British Parliament. After graduating from Cambridge University in 1806, Robert began his own training for political life. After practicing law for 20 years, he was elected to Parliament in 1826. There, one of his shining accomplishments was the introduction of a bill to remove restrictions placed on the Jews who lived in Great Britain during that time. A deeply spiritual man, Grant wrote several hymns, all of which were characterized by careful craftsmanship and colorful imagery. His classic text, "O Worship the King," is a paraphrase of Psalm 104. Originally the hymn contained two additional stanzas not included in modern hymnals:

The earth with its store of wonders untold,
Almighty, Thy power hath founded of old;
Hath stablished it fast by a changeless decree,
And round it hath cast, like a mantle, the sea.

O measureless Might, ineffable Love,
While angels delight to hymn Thee above,
Thy humbler creation, though feeble their lays,*
With true adoration shall sing to Thy praise.

In an interesting parallel to the life of Reginald Heber, who was appointed Bishop of Calcutta only to die three years later at the age of 43 (see "Holy, Holy, Holy"), Grant was named Governor of Bombay in 1834, and it was there that he died four years later, in 1838, at the age of 53.

LYONS
Robert Grant, 1833

Attr. to Johann Michael Haydn, 18th century

*Archaic term for "songs" or "anthems."
**Quoting G.F. Handel's "Allegro Maestoso" from *Water Music.*

2. O tell of His might, and sing of His grace,
   Whose robe is the light, whose canopy space.
   His chariots of wrath the deep thunderclouds form,
   And dark is His path on the wings of the storm.

3. Thy bountiful care, what tongue can recite?
   It breathes in the air; it shines in the light.
   It streams from the hills; it descends to the plain,
   And sweetly distills in the dew and the rain.

4. Frail children of dust, and feeble as frail,
   In Thee do we trust, nor find Thee to fail.
   Thy mercies so tender, how firm to the end!
   Our Maker, Defender, Redeemer, and Friend!

Oh, for a Thousand Tongues to Sing

Charles Wesley (1707-1788) and his brother John (1703-1791), sons of an Anglican minister (Samuel), both trained for ministry at Oxford University. While there, they were labeled (somewhat derisively) "methodists" because of the strict regimen of spiritual exercises and scholarship that they developed. After a short unsuccessful stint as missionaries to the Colonies–Georgia, specifically–they returned home to England, frustrated in their spiritual lives. In an interesting parallel to John Newton's life, it was during the sea voyage that seeds were planted, as they watched a group of Moravians experiencing amazing peace during rough seas. Shortly thereafter they experienced spiritual rebirth, and the rest is history–with John's preaching and Charles' hymnwriting becoming the catalyst for a great revival that swept across England.

Of all of Charles' more than 8,000 hymns, "Oh, for a Thousand Tongues to Sing" is perhaps his best-known. Originally a poem of 18 stanzas written on the first anniversary of his personal revival, it was first published in *Hymns and Sacred Poems* in 1740. It is believed to have been inspired by his Moravian friend, Peter Böhler, who had a recurring expression: "Had I a thousand tongues, I would praise Him with them all." In reality, Böhler's saying was most likely inspired by a German hymn published in 1704, which began with the same words: "O dass ich tausend zungen hätte." In 1780, the Wesley brothers published *Collection of Hymns for the People Called Methodists,* placing this hymn first in the book. And ever since, it has been the tradition to place it as the opening hymn in Methodist hymnals.

AZMON
Carl G. Gläser, 1828

Charles Wesley, 1739

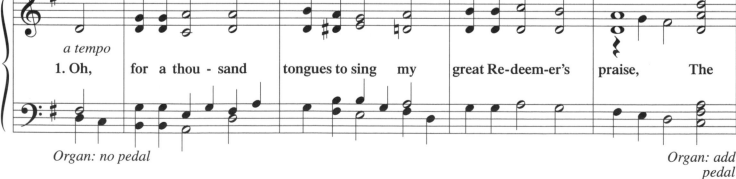

FJH2023

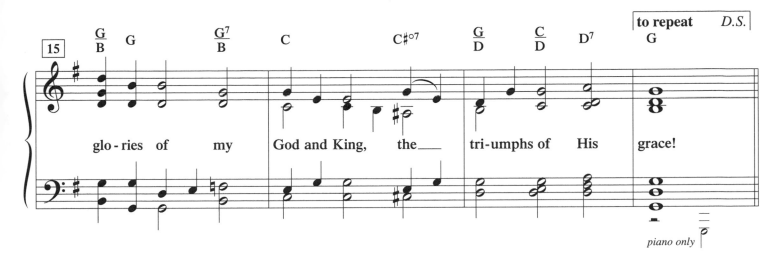

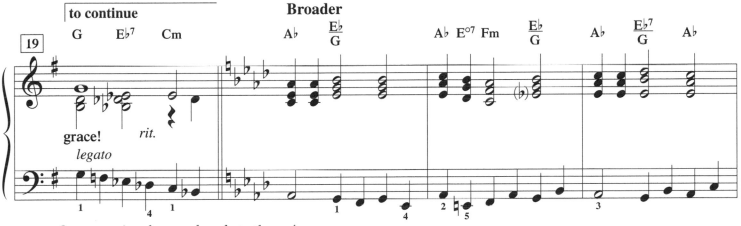

Organ: optional manuals only to the end

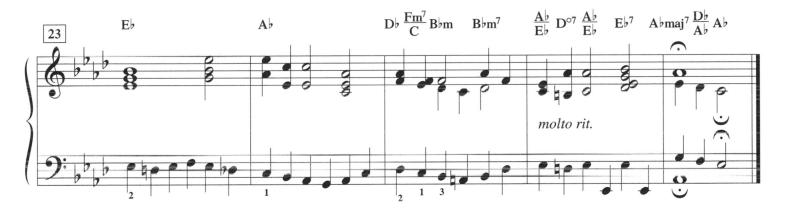

2. Jesus! the name that charms our fears,
That bids our sorrows cease;
'Tis music in the sinner's ears;
'Tis life and health and peace.

4. He speaks and, list'ning to his voice,
New life the dead receive.
The mournful, broken hearts rejoice;
The humble poor believe.

6. In Christ, your Head, ye then shall know,
Shall feel your sins forgiv'n,
Anticipate your heav'n below,
And own that love is heav'n.

3. He breaks the pow'r of cancelled sin;
He sets the pris'ner free.
His blood can make the foulest clean;
His blood availed for me.

5. Hear Him, ye deaf; His praise, ye dumb,
Your loosened tongues employ.
Ye blind, behold your Savior come;
And leap, ye lame, for joy.

7. My gracious Master and my God,
Assist me to proclaim,
To spread through all the earth abroad
The honors of Thy name.

FJH2023

Onward, Christian Soldiers

Down through the history of Christianity it has been customary to baptize new believers on Easter Sunday. But at some point, because of the cold weather in northern England, church leaders there began postponing the baptisms for 50 days, till Pentecost Sunday. Because of the white robes worn by the converts, the day was also known as White Sunday, or Whitsun. The celebration actually lasted through the next day–which was logically called Whitmonday or Whitmon.

In mid-19th century England, this religious holiday was traditionally observed in the Anglican Church with a "procession of witness"–children parading through the streets carrying banners, and following a leader who carried a cross. In 1864, as was the custom in the Horbury Bridge, Yorkshire parish, the children's procession was scheduled to march to a neighboring village on Whitmon, where they would attend a Sunday School rally. Their pastor, Sabine Baring-Gould (1834-1924), serving his first year at his first church, had a last-minute inspiration: their long walk would be less tiring if they had a suitable marching song to sing. The evening before, he scoured the church's hymnbook for something suitable, but found nothing. So laboring most of the night he crafted a text which he called "Hymn for Procession with Cross and Banners"–designing it to be sung to the theme of the slow movement of Haydn's *Symphony in D*, a familiar tune of the day. (Seven years later, in 1871, it was reset to the martial tune we know today by the famed English organist, Sir Arthur Seymour Sullivan, also known for his Victorian classic, "The Lost Chord.")

In 1868 Baring-Gould married Grace Taylor, the daughter of a poor wool mill worker, and that union eventually produced 15 children. In 1881, at the death of his father, he inherited a fortune. That same year he was appointed rector at Lew Trenchand, Devonshire. His new wealth allowed him to purchase a mansion–with plenty of room for his large family. There, he pastored the small parish, helped raise his children, and continued to write prolifically the rest of his life. Amazingly, he transcribed everything in longhand himself, without the assistance of a secretary. In addition to his own hymns (also including "Now the Day Is Over"), as well as those he translated, he produced an average of a novel a year for 52 years. Also noteworthy was his 15-volume *Lives of the Saints*, his *Curious Myths of the Middle Ages*, and his *Legends of the Old Testament*. He declared that he wrote as a discipline, not waiting for inspiration, but applying himself to the task until it was completed. The literary catalog of the British Museum lists more titles by him than any other author of his time. Yet ironically, after 90 years of life, with over 85 books written and 15 children successfully raised, he is best remembered for a children's marching song that he wrote one night as a 30-year-old bachelor.

ST. GERTRUDE
Arthur S. Sullivan, 1871

Sabine Baring-Gould, 1864

2. At the sign of triumph
Satan's host must flee;
On, then, Christian soldiers,
On to victory!
Hell's foundations quiver
At the shout of praise;
Christians, lift your voices,
Loud your anthems raise!
Onward, Christian soldiers...

3. Like a mighty army
Moves the Church of God.
Christians, we are treading
Where the saints have trod.
We are not divided;
All one body we:
One in hope and doctrine,
One in charity.
Onward, Christian soldiers...

4. Crowns and thrones may perish,
Kingdoms rise and wane;
But the Church of Jesus
Constant will remain.
Gates of hell can never
'Gainst that Church prevail;
We have Christ's own promise,
Which can never fail.
Onward, Christian soldiers...

5. Onward, then, ye people!
Join our happy throng;
Blend with us your voices
In the triumph song.
Glory, laud, and honor
Unto Christ the King:
This through countless ages
Men and angels sing.
Onward, Christian soldiers...

Praise to the Lord, the Almighty

Joachim Neander, born in 1650, came from a distinguished line of German clergymen. However, as a young college student Neander joined his peers in a wanton lifestyle that directly contradicted his upbringing. At the age of 20, he happened upon a service at St. Martin's Church, Bremen, where a new pastor, Theodore Under-Eyck, was speaking. Initially intending to scoff at the proceedings, Neander was so convicted by the powerful presentation of the Gospel that he instead remained to pray the prayer of a repentant prodigal. The following year, he launched into a teaching career which included tutoring students at the University of Heidelberg, and then serving as rector in a church-sponsored Latin School at Düsseldorf. At the age of 29, he returned to Bremen to serve as assistant to Under-Eyck at St. Martin's. Shortly thereafter he fell sick, and after several months died. However, he created several hymn texts in the last year of his brief life–most notably, "Praise to the Lord, the Almighty." It was written to fit an anonymous tune, LOBE DEN HERREN, which had first appeared in a hymnbook published 15 years earlier, in 1665–*Stralsund Gesangbuch.*

Catherine Winkworth (1829-1878) was born in London. Early in life she found her niche, when at the age of 26 she published her first collection of German hymns translated into English–*Lyra Germanica.* After 23 editions, and a sequel which had 12 editions, she followed with *Chorale Book for England,* 1863, which contained among other classics–"Praise to the Lord, the Almighty."

Joachim Neander, 1680
Tr. by Catherine Winkworth, 1863

LOBE DEN HERREN
Anonymous

2. Praise to the Lord, who o'er all things so wondrously reigneth,
Shelters thee under His wings, yea, so gently sustaineth!
Hast thou not seen
How thy desires all have been
Granted in what He ordaineth?

3. Praise to the Lord, who doth prosper thy work and defend thee;
Surely His goodness and mercy here daily attend thee.
Ponder anew
What the Almighty can do
If with His love He befriend thee.

4. Praise to the Lord! Oh, let all that is in me adore Him!
All that hath life and breath, come now with praises before Him!
Let the "amen"
Sound from His people again;
Gladly forever adore Him!

Rejoice, the Lord Is King

Charles Wesley (1707-1788) and his brother John (1703-1791), sons of an Anglican minister (Samuel), both trained for ministry at Oxford University. While there, they were labeled (somewhat derisively) "methodists" because of the strict regimen of spiritual exercises and scholarship that they developed. After a short unsuccessful stint as missionaries to the Colonies–Georgia, specifically–they returned home to England, frustrated in their spiritual lives. In an interesting parallel to John Newton's life, it was during the sea voyage that seeds were planted, as they watched a group of Moravians experiencing amazing peace during rough seas. Shortly thereafter they experienced spiritual rebirth, and the rest is history–with John's preaching and Charles' hymnwriting becoming the catalyst for a great revival that swept across England.

With Isaac Watts, Charles Wesley stands at the pinnacle of importance in the shaping of English hymnody. In his lifetime, no less than 6,500 hymns flowed from his pen. Besides "Rejoice, the Lord Is King," other Wesley hymns still in use today include "Hark! the Herald Angels Sing," "Love Divine, All Loves Excelling," "Jesus, Lover of My Soul," "A Charge to Keep I Have," "Arise, My Soul, Arise," "Come, Thou Long-Expected Jesus," "Soldiers of Christ, Arise," "Christ the Lord Is Risen Today," and "Oh, for a Thousand Tongues to Sing."

DARWALL
John Darwall, 1770

Charles Wesley, 1746

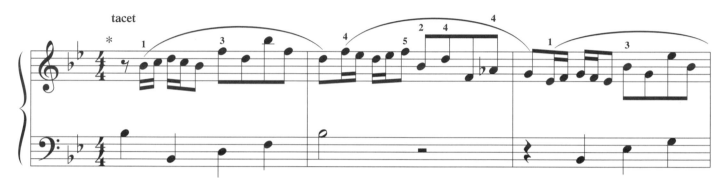

no organ or piano pedal throughout

*Quoting J.S. Bach's "Invention No. 14."

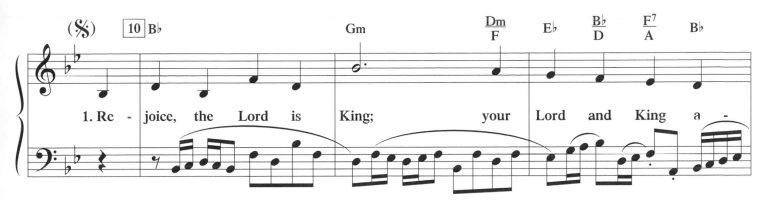

cued notes indicate vocal melody (not to be played by instruments)

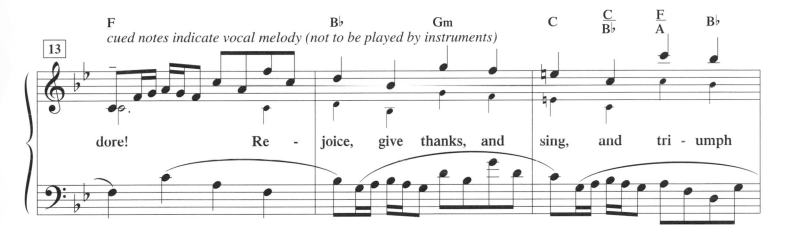

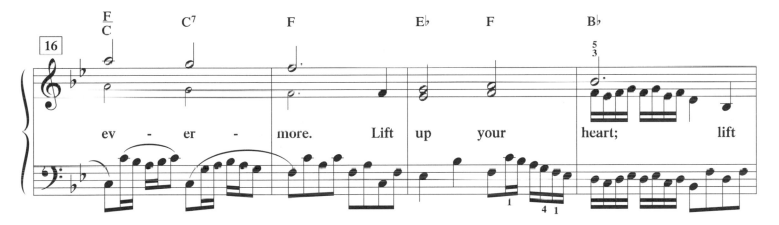

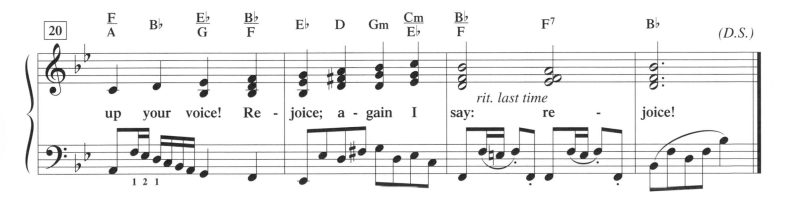

2. Jesus, the Savior, reigns,
   The God of truth and love.
   When He had purged our stains,
   He took His seat above.
   Lift up your heart;
   Lift up your voice!
   Rejoice; again I say: rejoice!

3. His kingdom cannot fail;
   He rules o'er earth and heav'n.
   The keys of death and hell
   Are to our Jesus giv'n.
   Lift up your heart;
   Lift up your voice!
   Rejoice; again I say: rejoice!

4. Rejoice in glorious hope!
   Our Lord, the Judge, shall come
   And take His servants up
   To their eternal home.
   Lift up your heart;
   Lift up your voice!
   Rejoice; again I say: rejoice!

Rejoice, Ye Pure in Heart

Edward Hayes Plumptre (1821-1891) was, in his day, among England's most distinguished ministers and educators. Ordained by the Anglican Church in 1846, he served in a long succession of posts–including college chaplain, dean, professor, rector, and vicar. He authored a number of books, including the definitive biography of Bishop Thomas Ken and several collections of poems and hymns. Of the latter, his most enduring are "Thine Arm, O Lord, in Days of Old" and "Rejoice, Ye Pure in Heart."

MARION
Edward H. Plumptre, 1865
Arthur H. Messiter, 1889

Slightly broader

Organ: no pedal. Play top notes of octaves only, on manuals

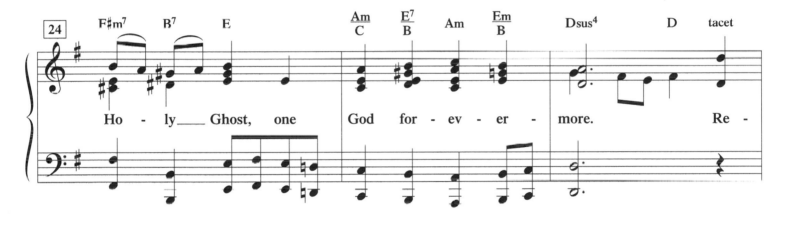

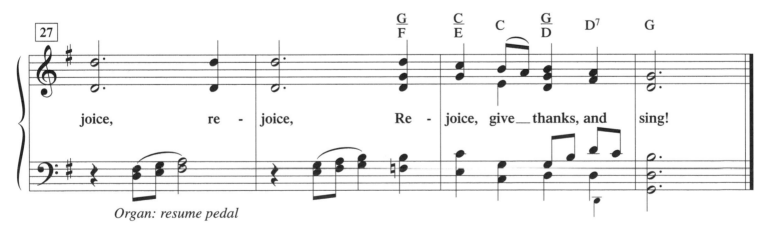

Organ: resume pedal

2. With all the angel choirs,
With all the saints on earth,
Pour out your strains of joy and bliss,
True rapture, noblest mirth!
Rejoice, rejoice,
Rejoice, give thanks, and sing!

3. Yes, on through life's long path,
Still chanting as ye go,
From youth to age, by night and day,
In gladness and in woe,
Rejoice, rejoice,
Rejoice, give thanks, and sing!

4. Still lift your standard high;
Still march in firm array.
As warriors, through the darkness toil
Till dawns the golden day.
Rejoice, rejoice,
Rejoice, give thanks, and sing!

FJH2023

Rock of Ages

The life of Augustus Montague Toplady has many amazing parallels to that of Henry Francis Lyte (see "Abide with Me"). Toplady was born in 1740 at Farnham, England. His father, a major in the British army, was killed the following year at the Siege of Cartagena (like the father of Henry F. Lyte, a captain, who died when Henry was just a toddler). Like the Lytes, the widow Toplady moved the family to Dublin. At the age of 16, Augustus attended an evangelistic service held in a barn, and there his heart was stirred and he dedicated himself to the service of God. Like Henry Lyte, Augustus was educated at Trinity College and was subsequently ordained by the Church of England at the age of 22. And like Lyte, he soon began to show symptoms of tuberculosis. "Rock of Ages" first appeared in 1776 in the *Gospel Magazine*, of which Toplady was editor. In that edition, Augustus wrote an article in which he attempted to show by mathematical computations how staggering is the sum total of sins committed by an individual in his lifetime, and how utterly impossible it would be for that individual to atone for this debt of guilt. However, he concluded, Christ, the sinner's refuge, has assumed the entire debt himself, and marked our accounts paid in full. Thus we can sing with confidence: "Rock of Ages, cleft for me..." And like Lyte and his poem "Abide with Me," Toplady's most famous contribution to hymnody turned out to be his swan song, for within two years the tuberculosis claimed another life, as he died in 1778 at the age of 38.

Augustus M. Toplady, 1776

TOPLADY
Thomas Hastings, 1830

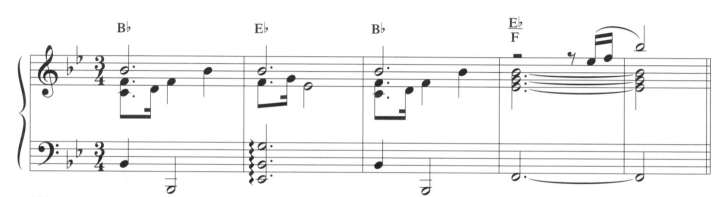

(this arrangement not recommended for use with organ)

1. Rock of A - ges, cleft for me, let me hide my-self in Thee. Let the
2. Could my tears for - ev - er flow, could my zeal no lan-guor know, These for

wat - er and the blood, from Thy wound - ed side which flowed, Be of
sin could not a - tone; Thou must save, and Thou a - lone. In my

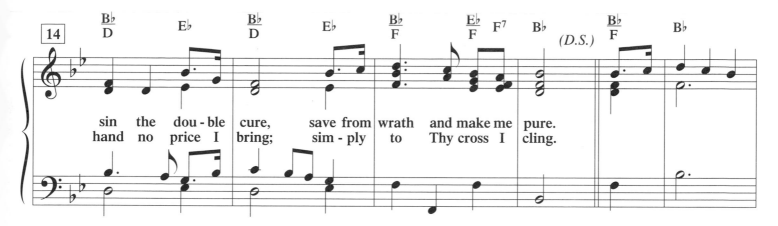

sin the dou-ble cure, save from wrath and make me pure.
hand no price I bring; sim-ply to Thy cross I cling.

3. While I draw this fleet-ing breath, When my

eyes shall close in death, When I rise to worlds un-known, And be-hold Thee on Thy

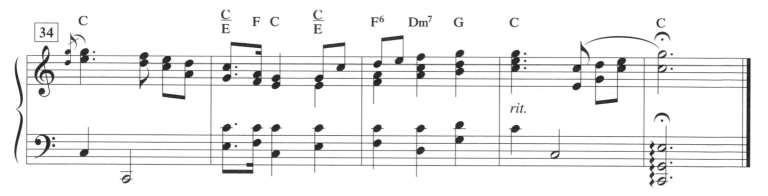

throne, Rock of A-ges, cleft for me, Let me hide my-self in Thee.

rit.

FJH2023

Savior, Like a Shepherd Lead Us

Dorothy Ann Thrupp (1779-1847) began her writing career by submitting poems to two London religious periodicals, using the pseudonym "Iota." In 1836 she edited a children's songbook, *Hymns for the Young*, which contained a good number of new hymn texts–all published anonymously. Thrupp was later credited as the author of most of the contents, including the hymn for which she is most remembered today–"Savior, Like a Shepherd Lead Us."

The American hymnal editor William Bradbury (1816-1868) wrote the tune which has become inextricably linked to this text, first introducing it in his 1859 Sunday School collection, *Oriola*. Bradbury, a protegé of the gifted composer Lowell Mason, also played an important role in encouraging others–including the blind poetess Fanny Crosby–to use their literary talents to create enduring hymn texts. Some other hymns for which he created the melodies include: "Just As I Am," "Sweet Hour of Prayer," "He Leadeth Me," "The Solid Rock," and "Jesus Loves Me."

BRADBURY

Attr. to Dorothy A. Thrupp, 1836

William B. Bradbury, 1859

131

2. We are Thine; do Thou befriend us,
   Be the Guardian of our way.
   Keep Thy flock; from sin defend us,
   Seek us when we go astray.
   Blessed Jesus, blessed Jesus!
   Hear, O hear us when we pray.
   Blessed Jesus, blessed Jesus!
   Hear, O hear us when we pray.

3. Thou hast promised to receive us,
   Poor and sinful though we be;
   Thou hast mercy to relieve us,
   Grace to cleanse, and pow'r to free.
   Blessed Jesus, blessed Jesus!
   Early let us turn to Thee.
   Blessed Jesus, blessed Jesus!
   Early let us turn to Thee.

4. Early let us seek Thy favor,
   Early let us do Thy will.
   Blessed Lord and only Savior,
   With Thy love our beings fill.
   Blessed Jesus, blessed Jesus!
   Thou hast loved us; love us still.
   Blessed Jesus, blessed Jesus!
   Thou hast loved us; love us still.

FJH2023

Silent Night, Holy Night

Franz Gruber was born in 1787 in a small hamlet in northern Austria, the son of poor weavers. Though his parents initially expected him to follow in their vocation, there was no denying his early musical aptitude. After studying both music and education, Gruber was granted a teaching position at Arnsdorf in 1807. Nine years later, in 1816, he took on a second job, assuming the duties of organist at a newly established parish church in Oberndorf, two miles away. Joseph Mohr was born in 1792 in Salzburg. Studying theology from childhood on, he was appointed assistant pastor at Oberndorf in 1817. Here, the theologian and teacher/organist became close confidants—so much so that Mohr felt comfortable in asking his colleague for a large favor: on the morning of December 24, 1818, he handed Gruber a poem he had written, with the request that the organist set it to a suitable melody arranged for two solo voices, chorus, and a guitar accompaniment. (While the choice of guitar may have been somewhat of an artistic decision, it was also a pragmatic one due to the fact that the organ was broken.) Later that same day Gruber completed the composition and it was performed in the Christmas Eve service that night, where it was received with great acclaim. The organ repairman present at the time, struck by the simple beauty of the song, carried it back home to the Zillerthal. Four sisters from that area, the Strassers, widely famous for their singing of local folk songs, heard the organ builder's rendition of "Stille Nacht." Immediately they added it to their repertoire, exposing it widely through their concert tours in the great cities of Europe. For many years, the origin of the song was unknown, as it went through several permutations. Most thought it to be just another folk song, while some speculated that it had been written by Michael Haydn. But in 1854, the royal court musicians in Berlin succeeded in tracing it back to the aging Franz Gruber, who on December 30 officially documented the details surrounding its creation and was proclaimed the rightful owner.

Joseph Mohr, 1818
Tr. of st. 1, 2, 4 by John F. Young, 1864
Tr. of st. 3: Anonymous

STILLE NACHT
Franz Gruber, 1818

(this arrangement not recommended for use with organ)

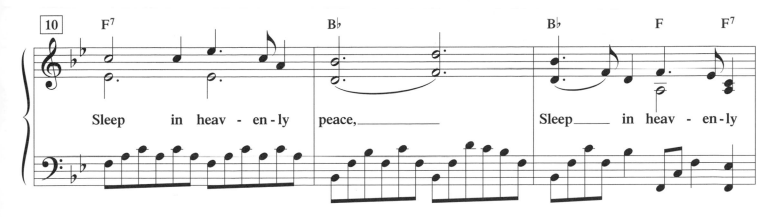

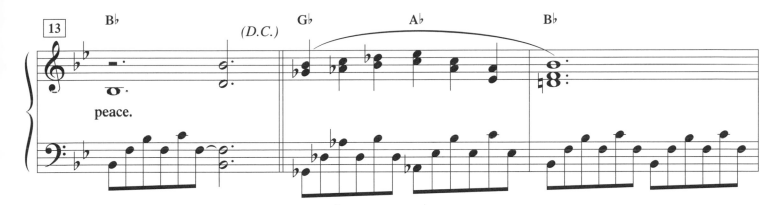

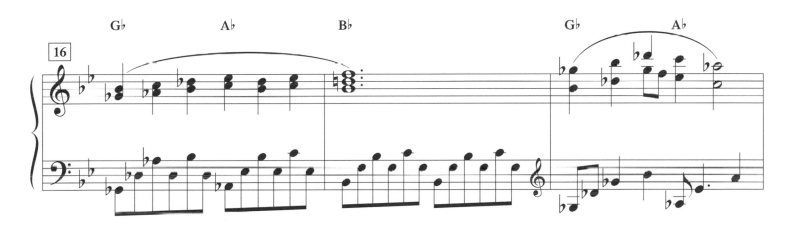

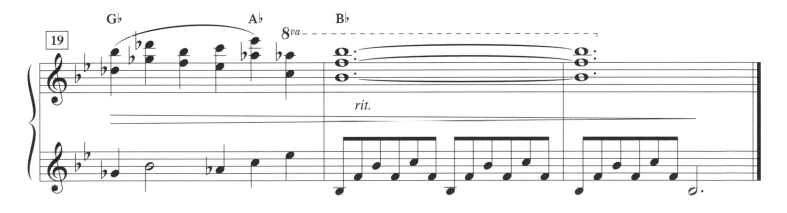

2. Silent night, holy night,
   Shepherds quake at the sight;
   Glories stream from heaven afar.
   Heav'nly hosts sing, "Alleluia!
   Christ the Savior is born!
   Christ the Savior is born!"

3. Silent night, holy night,
   Wondrous star, lend thy light.
   With the angels let us sing,
   Alleluia to our King.
   Christ the Savior is born,
   Christ the Savior is born.

4. Silent night, holy night,
   Son of God, love's pure light,
   Radiant beams from Thy holy face,
   With the dawn of redeeming grace,
   Jesus, Lord, at Thy birth,
   Jesus, Lord, at Thy birth.

FJH2023

Spirit of God, Descend Upon My Heart

George Croly was born in 1780 in Dublin, and it was there that he received his ministerial training and ordination by the Anglican Church. In 1810 he was appointed rector of two London churches–St. Benet and St. Stephen's–the latter one located among some of the worst slums of the city. Here he attracted large crowds, reviving a church that had been dormant for almost a century. When Croly's congregations expressed the desire for a hymnal, he set about to prepare one specifically for them. His resulting effort, *Psalms and Hymns for Public Worship,* included "Spirit of God, Descend Upon My Heart"–his only hymn to ever find universal acceptance, but one of the finest Pentecost prayers ever written. After a long career of pastoral ministry and writing, Croly died in 1860.

MORECAMBE
George Croly, 1854   Frederick C. Atkinson, 1870

(this arrangement not recommended for use with organ)

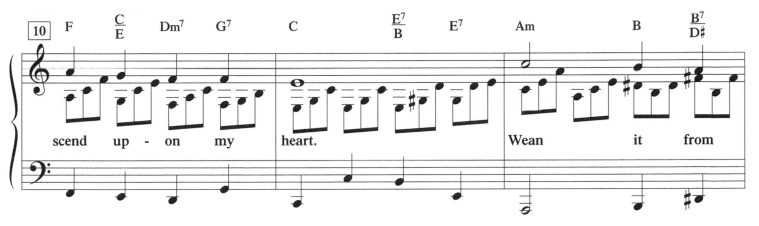

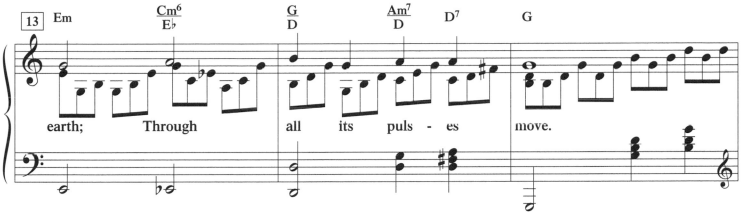

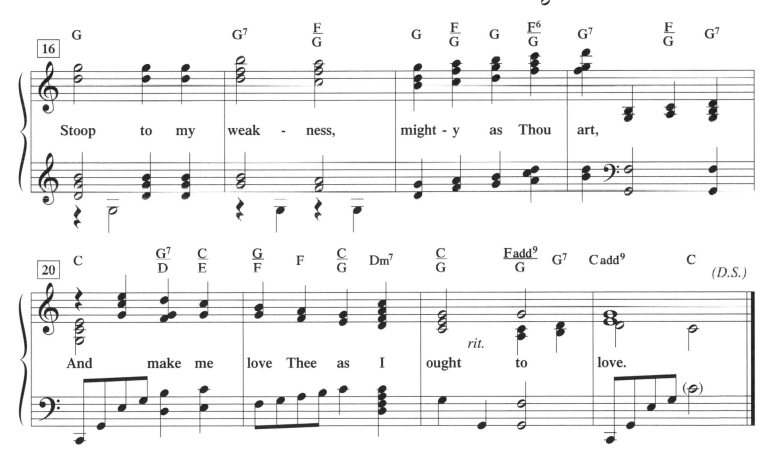

2. Hast Thou not bid us love Thee, God and King?
   All, all Thine own—soul, heart, and strength, and mind!
   I see Thy cross—there teach my heart to cling.
   O let me seek Thee, and O let me find!

3. I ask no dream, no prophet ecstacies,
   No sudden rending of the veil of clay,
   No angel visitant, no opening skies;
   But take the dimness of my soul away.

4. Teach me to feel that Thou art alway nigh.
   Teach me the struggles of the soul to bear,
   To check the rising doubt, the rebel sigh;
   Teach me the patience of unanswered prayer.

5. Teach me to love Thee as Thine angels love,
   One holy passion filling all my frame;
   The baptism of the heav'n-descended Dove,
   My heart an altar, and Thy love the flame.

Stand Up, Stand Up for Jesus

In 1858, three years before the outbreak of the Civil War, Philadelphia was swept by a great religious awakening known as "The Work of God in Philadelphia." The revival was fueled largely by the hard-hitting sermons of a young charismatic abolitionist Episcopal priest named Dudley Tyng. Four years earlier, at the age of 29, Tyng had become rector of the Church of the Epiphany in Philadelphia, succeeding his father. With two generations of ministers preceeding him and nurturing his faith, and with one degree from the University of Pennsylvania and another from the Episcopal Seminary at Alexandria, Virginia, Tyng came by his spiritual credentials honestly. However, it became obvious that he was not a good fit for the wealthy, culturally elite Epiphany congregation. Preaching that every single person was a sinner who needed to repent and be converted, and railing against the immorality of slavery, he soon found himself cross-current with the church leadership. So supported by some younger members of the parish, he had resigned from Epiphany and formed the Church of the Covenant, gathering in a small meeting hall. His family moved to the countryside outside of Philadelphia. In addition to his responsibilities at his new church, Tyng began giving noon lectures at the local YMCA. Interest grew almost exponentially, and hundreds, if not thousands, were converted. On one particularly memorable day–Tuesday, March 30, 1858–5,000 men gathered as the young firebrand preached from Exodus 10:11: "Ye that are men...serve the Lord." At the closing appeal, it was reported that 1,000 men believed, repented, and were converted. The next week, while home on the farm, Tyng took a study break to check on a mule-powered corn sheller. As he reached out to stroke the animal, his loose sleeve became entangled in the gears of the machine and his arm was severely mangled. Despite receiving the best medical attention available–which included amputation of the arm–he never recovered from the shock, and died within a week. But in his last lucid moments, he urged his doctor to become a Christian, he asked his wife to encourage their sons to be ministers, and he begged his father: "Stand up for Jesus...and tell my brethren of the ministry, wherever you meet them, to stand up for Jesus!" The following Sunday Tyng's friend and colleague, Rev. George Duffield, Jr., stood in his pulpit at Temple Presbyterian Church and preached from Ephesians 6:13-17, which begins: "Wherefore take unto you the whole armor of God, that ye may be able to withstand in the evil day, and having done all, to stand..." He concluded his sermon with a poem– "Stand Up, Stand Up for Jesus"–that he had written after hearing of his friend's last words at the funeral that week. His Sunday School superintendent printed the words in a leaflet for distribution to his students. One of the leaflets came to the attention of the publishers of a Baptist periodical, *The Church Psalmist,* where it was published in 1859. From there it found its way into hymnals, set to a tune written a couple of decades earlier by composer George Webb for a secular song. Though written with spiritual warfare in mind, a few years later as the nation was ripped in half by armed conflict, it became part of the standard repertoire sung around Union army campfires.

WEBB

George Duffield, Jr., 1858

George J. Webb, 1837

2. Stand up, stand up for Jesus.
   The trumpet call obey;
   Forth to the mighty conflict
   In this, His glorious day.
   Ye who are men, now serve Him
   Against unnumbered foes;
   Let courage rise with danger,
   And strength to strength oppose.

3. Stand up, stand up for Jesus;
   Stand in His strength alone.
   The arm of flesh will fail you,
   Ye dare not trust your own.
   Put on the gospel armor
   And, watching unto prayer,
   Where duty calls or danger,
   Be never wanting there.

4. Stand up, stand up for Jesus.
   The strife will not be long;
   This day the noise of battle,
   The next, the victor's song.
   To him who overcometh
   A crown of life shall be;
   He with the King of Glory
   Shall reign eternally.

The Church's One Foundation

Samuel John Stone was born in the London area in 1839. Following his graduation from Oxford University, he spent his life ministering to the poor and underprivileged of London's East Side, where it was later said of him: "He created a beautiful place of worship for the humble folk, and made it a center of light in the dark places." Always looking to meet the needs around him, Stone renovated one of his church buildings and opened it at 6:30 a.m. as a resting place for the crowds of workers who had nowhere else to go between the arrival of their commuter trains and the opening of their offices. "The Church's One Foundation" was written in response to a religious controversy which was shaking the Anglican Church to its roots. Stone weighed in on the issue, defending the orthodox faith against an offending bishop and others of his ilk who were promoting "Higher Criticism"–all of whom he referred to as "false sons in her pale." The hymn text, set to a tune composed two years earlier, became the battle cry for the conservatives of the church–with its pointed warnings against heresy. Through subsequent generations, the hymn's role has evolved–serving more to unite than to divide as hymnal editors have removed the original "attack stanzas." Today's version calls Christians from every tradition to celebrate the unity of the Church as demonstrated by their common belief in "one Lord, one faith, one birth."

AURELIA
Samuel S. Wesley, 1864

Samuel J. Stone, 1866

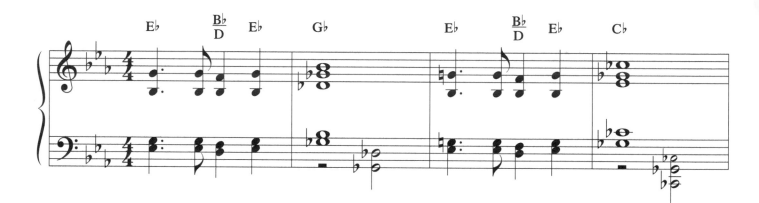

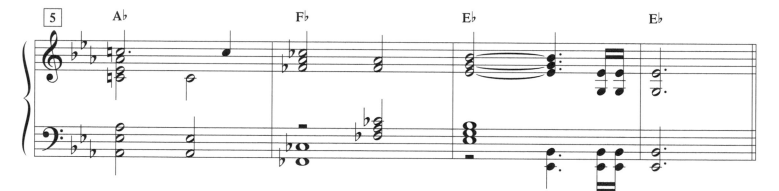

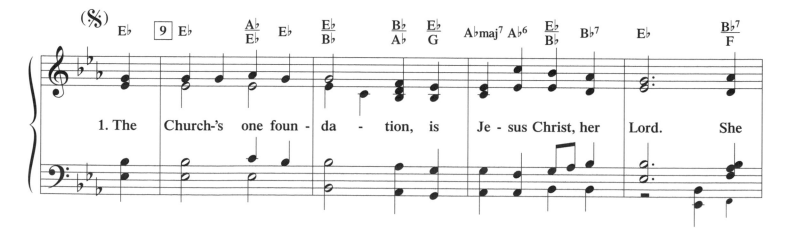

1. The Church-'s one foun - da - tion, is Je - sus Christ, her Lord. She

2. Elect from ev'ry nation,
   Yet one o'er all the earth;
   Her charter of salvation:
   One Lord, one faith, one birth.
   One holy name she blesses;
   Partakes one holy food;
   And to one hope she presses,
   With ev'ry grace endued.

3. 'Mid toil and tribulation,
   And tumult of her war,
   She waits the consummation
   Of peace forevermore;
   Till, with the vision glorious,
   Her longing eyes are blessed,
   And the great Church victorious
   Shall be the Church at rest.

4. Yet she on earth hath union
   With God, the Three in One,
   And mystic, sweet communion
   With those whose rest is won.
   Oh, happy ones and holy!
   Lord, give us grace that we,
   Like them, the meek and lowly,
   On high may dwell with Thee.

The First Noel

This Christmas poem has obscure roots, possibly dating back to the Miracle Plays of the 13th and 14th centuries. Likewise, the melody originated in antiquity, either in England or France. Text and tune were first brought together in William Sandys' 1833 collection, *Christmas Carols, Ancient and Modern.* The harmonization commonly found in hymnals today was arranged in 1871 by Sir John Stainer, who is best remembered for his cantata, *The Crucifixion,* with its classic choral piece, "God So Loved the World."

"Noel" is the French word for Christmas, and is derived from the Latin "natalis," meaning "birthday."

THE FIRST NOEL
Traditional Melody

Traditional English Carol

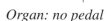

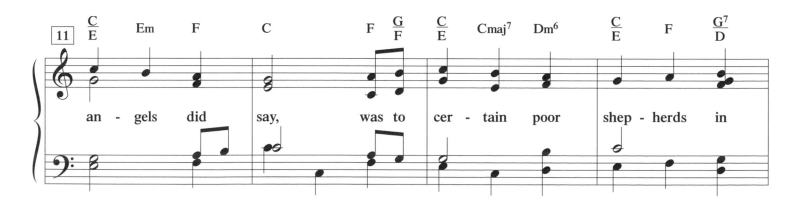

2. They looked up and saw a star
   Bright in the east beyond them far;
   And to the earth it gave great light,
   And so it continued both day and night.
   Noel...

3. And by the light of that same star
   Three wise men came from country far;
   To seek for a King was their intent,
   And to follow the star where'er it went.
   Noel...

4. This star drew nigh to the northwest;
   O'er Bethlehem it took its rest.
   And there it did both stop and stay
   Right over the place where Jesus lay.
   Noel...

5. Then entered in those wise men three,
   Full rev'rently upon the knee,
   And offered there, in His presence,
   Their gold and myrrh and frankincense.
   Noel...

This Is My Father's World

Maltbie Davenport Babcock was born in 1858 in Syracuse, New York. Tall and muscular, he distinguished himself as a multi-sport athlete at Syracuse University. After graduate studies at Auburn Theological Seminary, he was ordained a minister in the Presbyterian Church, eventually succeeding Henry van Dyke at the well-known Brick Presbyterian Church in New York City. (See "Joyful, Joyful, We Adore Thee" for more about van Dyke.) Babcock, like his predecessor, was a great lover of nature; ironically, both ministers are remembered primarily for one great hymn each–both paeans to the splendor of creation. In 1901, the year that "This Is My Father's World" was written, Babcock and his wife were returning home from a trip to the Holy Land when he died unexpectedly in Naples, Italy, at the age of 43. Among his other hymns–most of which were published after his death–was a challenge such as one would expect from the athletic, manly preacher that he was: "Be Strong."

Be strong!
We are not here to play, to dream, to drift.
We have hard work to do, and loads to lift.
Shun not the struggle; face it. 'Tis God's gift.

Be strong!
Say not the days are evil–who's to blame?
And fold the hands and acquiesce–oh, shame!
Stand up, speak out, and bravely–in God's name.

Be strong!
It matters not how entrenched the wrong,
How hard the battle goes, the day, how long.
Faint not, fight on! Tomorrow comes the song.

TERRA BEATA
Traditional English Melody

Maltbie D. Babcock, 1901

Organ: no pedal

Organ: resume pedal
(beat 4)

This is my Fa-ther's world. I__ rest me in the thought, Of

rocks and trees, of__ skies and seas, His hand__ the__ won-ders__ wrought.

tacet to the end

(mel.)

Organ: no pedal

molto rit.

Organ: pedal

2. This is my Father's world.
   The birds their carols raise.
   The morning light, the lily white
   Declare their Maker's praise.
   This is my Father's world.
   He shines in all that's fair.
   In the rustling grass I hear Him pass;
   He speaks to me ev'rywhere.

3. This is my Father's world.
   Oh, let me ne'er forget
   That though the wrong seems oft so strong
   God is the Ruler yet.
   This is my Father's world.
   The battle is not done;
   Jesus, who died, shall be satisfied,
   And earth and heav'n be one.

FJH2023

To God Be the Glory

Fanny Crosby (1820-1915) was rendered sightless while a baby because of a physician's error. Rather than considering her handicap an affliction, she deemed it a blessing, saying, "When I get to heaven, the first face that shall ever gladden my sight will be that of my Savior." This amazing lady is thought to have written 8,000 hymn texts in her lifetime, many of which are still found in hymnals today. One of her best-loved hymns, "To God Be the Glory," received its first widespread exposure when the American evangelist, D.L. Moody–along with his songleader, Ira D. Sankey– took it to Great Britain in 1873. The next year, Sankey included it in *Sacred Songs and Solos,* a hymn collection published in England. But for some unknown reason, he failed to include it in his landmark series, *Gospel Hymns,* published upon his return to America in 1875. And so, while somewhat well-known in Great Britain, it languished in relative obscurity in its home country for many years. In 1952, Cliff Barrows of the Billy Graham evangelistic team discovered it during a visit to England, and included it in a songbook being compiled for the upcoming London crusade of 1954. Graham was impressed by how enthusiastically the audience sang it, and so made it the crusade theme song–having it sung every night. Returning to America, his team used it in their 1954 Nashville crusade, where it met with a similar rousing response. From there it was quickly embraced by many denominations and began showing up in new hymnals.

Fanny J. Crosby, ca. 1873

TO GOD BE THE GLORY
William H. Doane, ca. 1873

2. Oh, perfect redemption, the purchase of blood,
To ev'ry believer, the promise of God!
The vilest offender who truly believes,
That moment from Jesus a pardon receives.

Praise the Lord! Praise the Lord!...

3. Great things He hath taught us, great things He hath done,
And great our rejoicing through Jesus, the Son!
But purer and higher and greater will be
Our wonder, our vict'ry when Jesus we see!

Praise the Lord! Praise the Lord!...

FJH2023

We Gather Together

The hymn text later translated as "We Gather Together" was probably written around 1597, though its author and precise date of creation is unknown. It first appeared in 1626 in a book entitled *Nederlandtsche Gedenck-clanck*, a history of the Netherlands' long struggle for independence from Spain. This chronicle, complete with songs and illustrations, was the work of one Adrianus Valerius, a Dutch renaissance man renowned as a musician, a poet, a historian, and a lawyer. For over 200 years, the song was primarily known only to the Dutch people–used as a patriotic song, a reminder of their heritage. In 1877 Edward Kremser, a Viennese conductor and composer, happened upon the tune combined with a German translation of the text, and was inspired to arrange it for male chorus. In a form very close to its current appearance in hymnals, he included it in a published collection of six Dutch folk songs, *Sechs Altniederlandische Volkslieder*. From Austria, the collection found its way to Milwaukee, Wisconsin around 1895, where it became a favorite resource for the choral societies in the German-speaking immigrant community.

Theodore Baker (1851-1934) was a well-respected music scholar who, though a New Yorker by birth, had received his postgraduate music education at the University of Leipzig. In 1892, he began what would turn out to be a 34-year career as an editor for G. Schirmer, Inc. A brilliant linguist, he translated many German and French music textbooks. However, he is probably best known for his dictionaries of musicians and musical terms, still in print today. In 1894, he translated "We Gather Together" into English, but it didn't become well-known until it was included in a collection entitled *Dutch Folk Songs* (1917).

Dutch Folk Hymn, 16th century
Tr. by Theodore Baker, 1894

KREMSER
Dutch Folk Tune

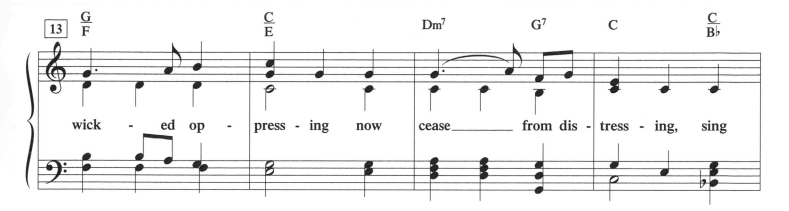

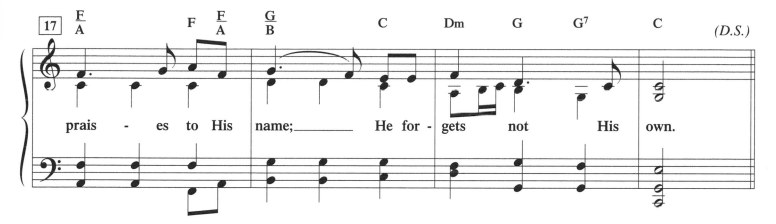

2. Beside us to guide us, our God with us joining,
   Ordaining, maintaining His kingdom divine;
   So from the beginning the fight we were winning.
   Thou, Lord, wast at our side; all glory be Thine.

3. We all do extol Thee, Thou Leader triumphant,
   And pray that Thou still our Defender wilt be.
   Let Thy congregation escape tribulation.
   Thy name be ever praised; O Lord, make us free!

Were You There

*The Africans who were brought to the American South on slave ships were very musical people, accustomed to expressing religious ideas in song. Sometimes they would pick up pieces of hymns or biblical text–perhaps by waiting outside the churches–and would incorporate these words and melodies into their songs. Biblical stories such as Daniel in the lions' den, the Israelites' slavery in Egypt, and the sufferings of Christ–they all spoke powerful messages of hope to those who were oppressed. Sometimes the songs were created as a way of pouring out to God their deepest prayers, desires, and frustrations.

The slaves would sing while working all day, and then would often meet at night, sometimes secretly for fear of punishment, where they would improvise in song and dance for hours, even after a hard day's work. These were songs of survival, songs that gave the courage to go on living when life seemed to be nothing but pain. They were created all throughout the 200 years of slavery, although they weren't known to most Americans until the latter half of the 19th century. "Were You There?" is one of these "spirituals"–as they became known–which has taken its place in standard hymnody.

When the Civil War ended in 1865, there was an overabundance of unwanted army brass band instruments. The newly-emancipated slaves picked them up and incorporated them into their music. Following the African tradition of honoring the dead, they would make music on the way to and from the burial. In New Orleans this developed into the marching band tradition at funerals. From this came the evolution of ragtime and the many other forms of jazz. Starting in New Orleans, jazz moved to Chicago, Kansas City, New York, and beyond. Worldwide, jazz is one of America's most popular exports.

WERE YOU THERE
Traditional Spiritual

Traditional Spiritual

*From the foreword to Teresa Wilhelmi's FJH piano collection, *Poor Wayfaring Stranger*, FF1424.

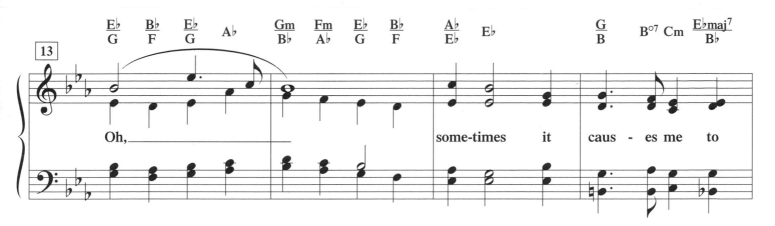

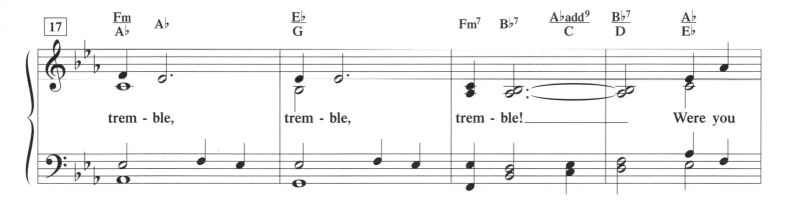

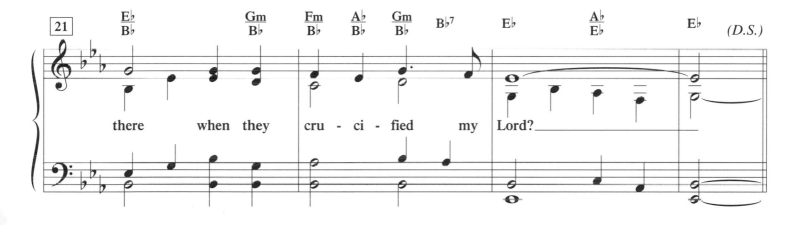

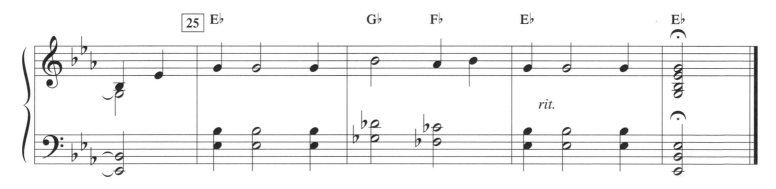

2. Were you there when they nailed Him to a tree?
   Were you there when they nailed Him to a tree?
   Oh, sometimes it causes me to tremble, tremble, tremble!
   Were you there when they nailed Him to a tree?

3. Were you there when they laid Him in a tomb?
   Were you there when they laid Him in a tomb?
   Oh, sometimes it causes me to tremble, tremble, tremble!
   Were you there when they laid Him in a tomb?

4. Were you there when He rose up from the dead?
   Were you there when He rose up from the dead?
   Oh, sometimes it causes me to tremble, tremble, tremble!
   Were you there when He rose up from the dead?

What a Friend We Have in Jesus

The story behind "What a Friend We Have in Jesus" is an example of beauty coming out of tragedy. Its author, Joseph Scriven, was born in Dublin, Ireland in 1820, where he graduated from Trinity College. Anticipating a career as an army officer, he next spent several years in a military college. When poor health prohibited him from pursuing that goal further, he took up theology, studying for the Anglican ministry. Then the night before he was to be married, his fiancée drowned in a freak accident in which she was thrown from a horse into a river. Shortly thereafter, Scriven emigrated to Ontario, Canada where, after some time, he fell in love again. But in another cruel twist of fate, his second fiancée died of pneumonia shortly after being baptized in a freezing cold lake. By most accounts, Scriven wrote his famous poem at this point in his life, in 1857. He sent one copy–along with the news of his latest misfortune–to his mother still living in Ireland, and kept another copy in his own scrapbook. He never married, but spent the rest of his life doing some tutoring, but mostly menial labor–primarily handyman work for widows and others too poor to hire help. Though shadowed by a cloud of melancholy all his life, and increasingly viewed as eccentric, he was also known for a deep Christian faith which was demonstrated by the sacrificial giving of his time and meager possessions to those in need. During an illness, he was visited by a neighbor who ran across the unsigned poem as he leafed through Scriven's scrapbooks. When pressed for details, the modest Irishman is quoted as saying, "The Lord and I wrote it between us." The neighbor sent a copy of the poem to a Boston publisher and it soon appeared in an 1865 collection, *Social Hymns, Original and Selected.* From there the poem found its way into a Sunday School song collection entitled *Silver Wings,* published in Richmond, Virginia in 1870. Here it was set to music by Charles C. Converse, an American lawyer and inventor who had earlier in life studied classical music in Germany, where he counted Franz Liszt and Louis Spohr among his friends. In 1875, Ira Sankey discovered the hymn and made it the last addition to a collection on which Philip P. Bliss and he were collaborating, *Gospel Hymns No. 1.* Later, when reflecting on the hymn's meteoric rise in popularity, Sankey wrote, "The last hymn that went into the book became one of the first in favor." Sadly, the hymn's success didn't translate into happiness for Scriven. In 1886, at the age of 66, he was severely depressed over health and financial issues. In October of that year, while feverish and possibly delirious, he wandered down to a nearby lake where he was found the next morning drowned in six inches of water. Accident or suicide–no one is quite sure. But because he was so well-loved and respected in his community, a monument with the hymn inscribed was erected in his honor on a highway running north from Lake Ontario.

CONVERSE
Charles C. Converse, 1868

Joseph M. Scriven, 1857

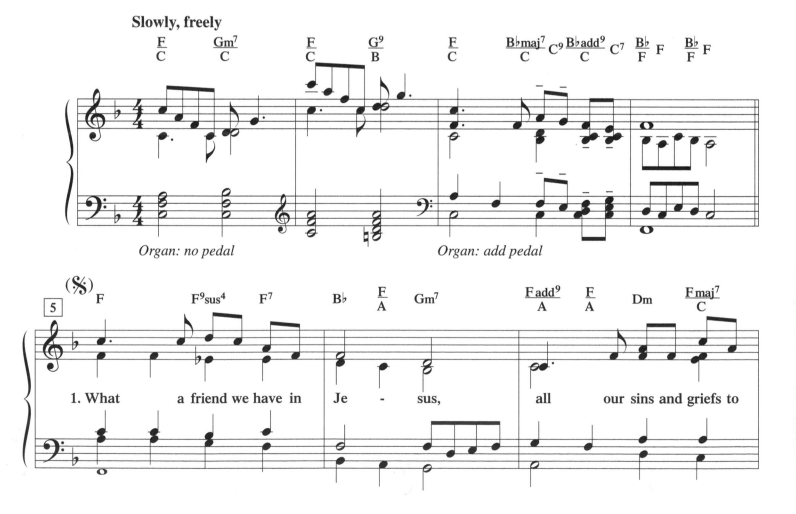

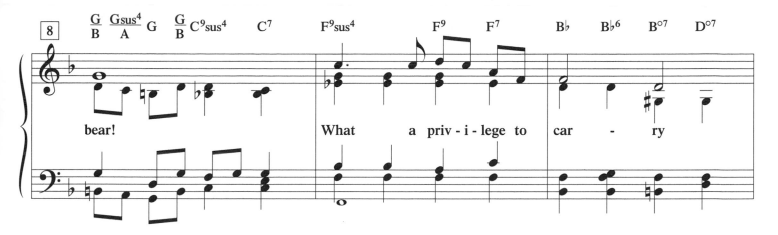

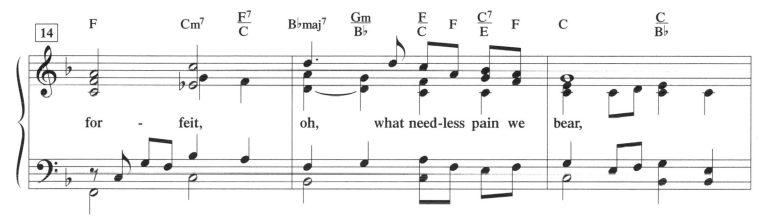

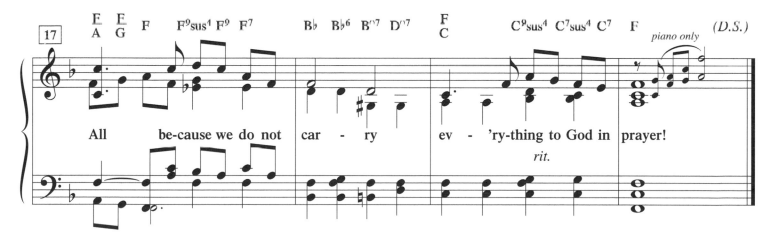

2. Have we trials and temptations?
   Is there trouble anywhere?
   We should never be discouraged;
   Take it to the Lord in prayer.
   Can we find a friend so faithful
   Who will all our sorrows share?
   Jesus knows our ev'ry weakness;
   Take it to the Lord in prayer.

3. Are we weak and heavy-laden,
   Cumbered with a load of care?
   Precious Savior, still our Refuge!
   Take it to the Lord in prayer.
   Do thy friends despise, forsake thee?
   Take it to the Lord in prayer.
   In His arms He'll take and shield thee;
   Thou wilt find a solace there.

What Child Is This

The hymn text, "What Child Is This" was written by an Englishman, William Chatterton Dix (1837-1898). Originally part of a longer poem entitled "The Manger Throne," the three stanzas which form the carol as we know it today were culled out and set to the traditional English tune, GREENSLEEVES, in 1865. Writing verse was an avocation for Dix; his "day job" involved managing a Glasgow-based marine insurance company. He came by his love of poetry honestly, however, as evidenced by the fact that his father, a surgeon, had written the biography of Thomas Chatterton, a famous poet from Dix's home town of Bristol. During his lifetime, Dix published four collections of hymns. Other texts of his which are still found in hymnals include "As with Gladness Men of Old" and "Alleluia, Sing to Jesus."

The tune, GREENSLEEVES, has a long history, first showing up around 1580. Legend has it that it was written by Henry VIII. It was well-known in the days of Shakespeare, as he mentions it twice in *The Merry Wives of Windsor*. The four-part setting found in many hymnals today was arranged in 1871 by Sir John Stainer, best known for his cantata, *The Crucifixion*.

GREENSLEEVES
William C. Dix, 1865   Traditional English Melody, 16th century

2. Why lies he in such mean estate
   Where ox and ass are feeding?
   Good Christian, fear; for sinners here
   The silent Word is pleading.

   This, this is Christ, the King...

3. So bring Him incense, gold, and myrrh;
   Come, peasant, king to own Him.
   The King of Kings salvation brings;
   Let loving hearts enthrone Him.

   This, this is Christ, the King...

What Wondrous Love Is This

"What Wondrous Love Is This" is an American folk hymn of unknown authorship, no doubt passed along by oral tradition for many years. It was first documented in 1835, when it appeared in William Walker's *Southern Harmony*. The text expounds on Galatians 3:13: Christ hath redeemed us from the curse of the law, being made a curse for us; for it is written, "Cursed is every one that hangeth on a tree." Stanzas 3 and 4 look ahead to the scenes of multitudes worshipping around the great white throne, as depicted in *Revelations*. The Dorian mode of the tune gives it a sense of awe and mystery appropriate for dealing with the wonder of the Atonement.

American Folk Hymn

WONDROUS LOVE
American Folk Tune

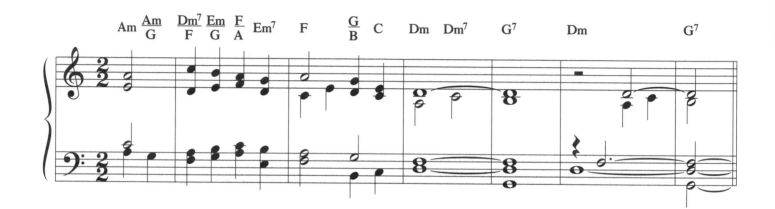

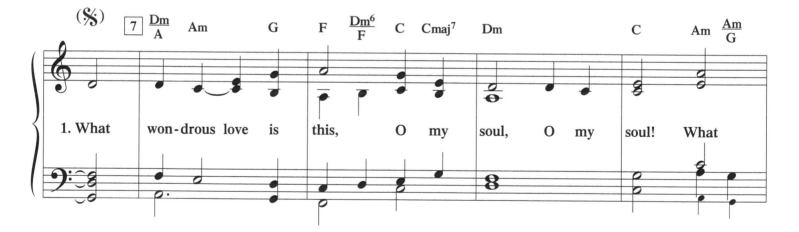

1. What won-drous love is this, O my soul, O my soul! What

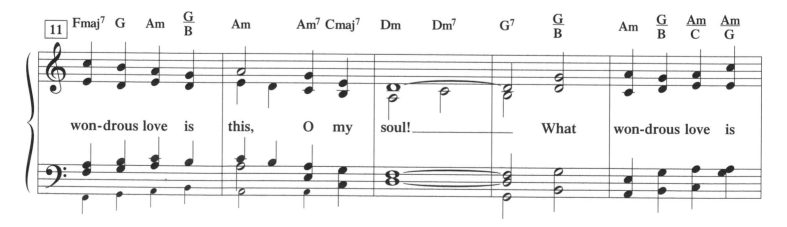

won-drous love is this, O my soul!____ What won-drous love is

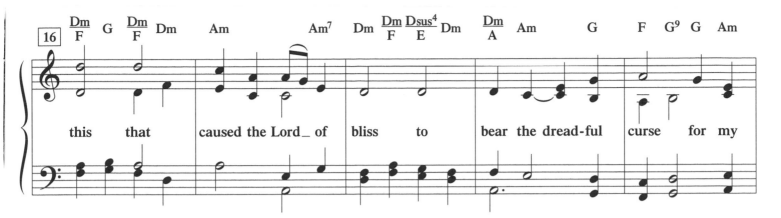

this that caused the Lord _ of bliss to bear the dread-ful curse for my

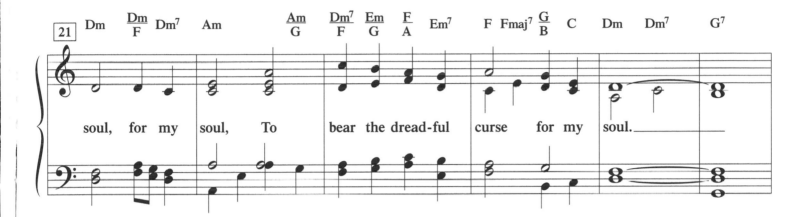

soul, for my soul, To bear the dread-ful curse for my soul._____

2. When I was sinking down,
   Sinking down, sinking down,
   When I was sinking down, sinking down,
   When I was sinking down
   Beneath God's righteous frown,
   Christ laid aside His crown
   For my soul, for my soul,
   Christ laid aside His crown for my soul.

3. To God and to the Lamb
   I will sing, I will sing.
   To God and to the Lamb I will sing.
   To God and to the Lamb
   Who is the great I Am,
   While millions join the theme,
   I will sing, I will sing.
   While millions join the theme, I will sing.

4. And when from death I'm free,
   I'll sing on, I'll sing on.
   And when from death I'm free, I'll sing on.
   And when from death I'm free,
   I'll sing and joyful be,
   And through eternity,
   I'll sing on, I'll sing on.
   And through eternity, I'll sing on.

When I Survey the Wondrous Cross

Born into a Puritan home in Southampton, England, Watts was quite sickly, yet very precocious. Starting with a study of Latin at the age of 4, he added Greek at age 9, French at age 11, and Hebrew at age 13. It is said that young Isaac was prone to converse in rhyme, to the point of tiring his parents. At one point, in an effort to enforce a prohibition on his poetic chatter, his father resorted to a spanking. As the anecdote goes, even then the youngster cried through his tears:

"O Father, do some pity take,
And I will no more verses make."

At that time, the music in the Congregational Church consisted of strict and rather stilted settings of the Book of Psalms, "lined out" by the precentor and repeated by the congregation. Watts, 18 at the time, is quoted as saying, "The singing of God's praise is the part of worship nighest heaven, and its performance among us is the worst on earth." At this, his father, a deacon, challenged him to give the Church something better. Isaac accepted the challenge, and though it seemed presumptuous at the time wrote his first hymn, which was introduced in the following Sunday evening service. The congregation enthusiastically accepted Watts' initial effort and encouraged him to write others. With great fervor, he plunged into the task. Two years later, he published a collection, *Hymns and Spiritual Songs,* containing 210 hymns, the vast majority of which were his. Twelve years later, he published a metrical version of the *Psalter*, in which the Old Testament psalms were paraphrased in New Testament language, or "Christianized."

Watts became a minister in the Reformed Church, serving the Mark Lane Independent Church in London until his frail health forced him to resign. At that point, he was compelled by Sir Thomas and Lady Abney to reside in their home. This visit turned into a 36-year stay for the physically disabled, yet mentally brilliant Watts. In this comfortable and happy environment, he continued to write hymns to the end of his life. The 600-plus hymns which flowed from his pen earned him the posthumous title, "the father of English hymnody."

There are two tunes most commonly associated with "When I Survey the Wondrous Cross"–ROCKINGHAM and HAMBURG. The latter is best known in America, and was written in 1824 by Lowell Mason while living in Savannah, Georgia. The solemn, simple melody is based on Gregorian chant and uses only five notes.

HAMBURG
Isaac Watts, 1707
Lowell Mason, 1824

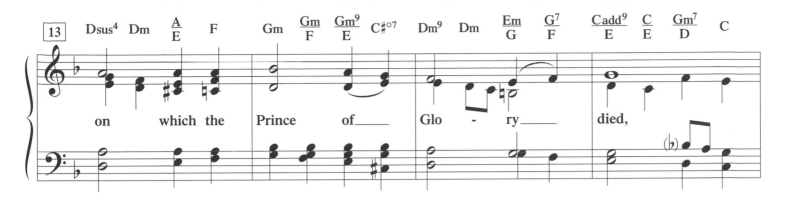

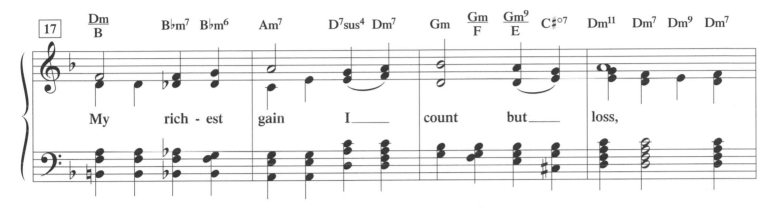

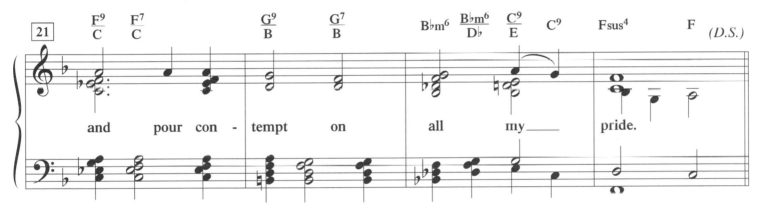

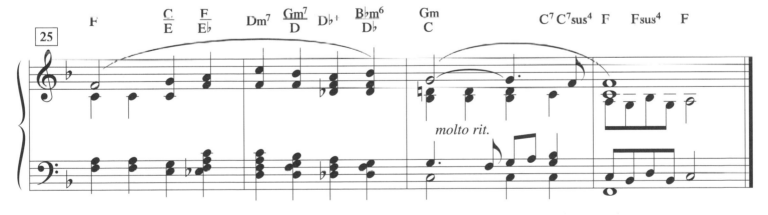

2. Forbid it, Lord, that I should boast,
   Save in the death of Christ, my God.
   All the vain things that charm me most,
   I sacrifice them to His blood.

3. See, from His head, His hands, His feet,
   Sorrow and love flow mingled down.
   Did e'er such love and sorrow meet,
   Or thorns compose so rich a crown.

4. Were the whole realm of nature mine,
   That were a present far too small.
   Love so amazing, so divine,
   Demands my soul, my life, my all!

FJH2023

158

When Morning Gilds the Skies

The anonymous German hymn text, "Beim frühen Morgenlicht," translated in 1854 by Edward Caswell as "When Morning Gilds the Skies," was originally published in *Katholisches Gesangbuch*, Würzburg, in 1828.

The tune LAUDES DOMINI was composed especially for this text by Sir Joseph Barnby (1838-1896), and first appeared in *Hymns Ancient and Modern*, London, 1868. Joseph, son of organist Thomas Barnby, was immersed in church music from birth, gaining proficiency in both singing and organ playing while still a child. At the age of 16, he entered the Royal Academy of Music in London. Two years later, Barnby competed for the first Mendelssohn Scholarship. When the examinations were over, of the nineteen applicants, he was tied for first place with Arthur Sullivan. (After a second test, Sullivan won.) Barnby was organist for many years in some of the most prestigious churches of his time, during which time he also orchestrated and conducted major concerts. In 1878, he helped found the London Music Society, becoming its first director and conductor. In 1892, at the age of 54, he was knighted and also appointed Principal of the Guildhall School of Music. Barnby's compositions include an oratorio, *Rebekah*, 1870, and a large number of hymn tunes, anthems, and vocal solos. In addition, he edited five hymnals, the most influential of which was *The Hymnary* (1872).

Anonymous German Hymn, 1828
Tr. by Edward Caswell, 1854

LAUDES DOMINI
Joseph Barnby, 1868

FJH2023

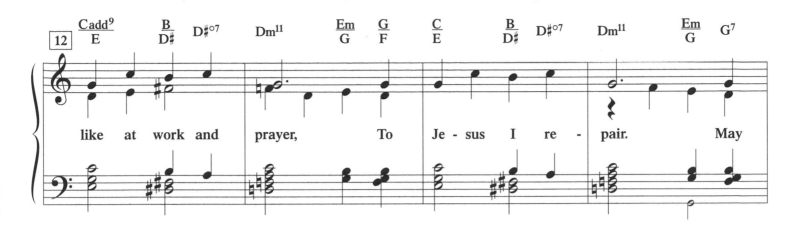

like at work and prayer, To Je-sus I re-pair. May

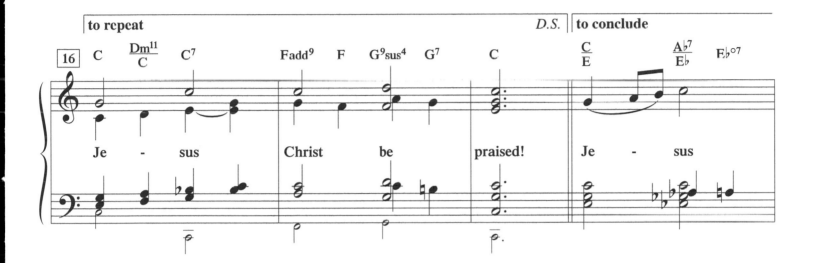

to repeat   D.S. | to conclude

Je - sus Christ be praised! Je - sus

Christ_____ be praised!_____

rit.

2. Does sadness fill my mind?
 A solace here I find:
 May Jesus Christ be praised!
 Or fades my earthly bliss?
 My comfort still is this:
 May Jesus Christ be praised!

3. The night becomes as day
 When from the heart we say:
 May Jesus Christ be praised!
 The pow'rs of darkness fear
 When this sweet chant they hear:
 May Jesus Christ be praised!

4. Ye nations of mankind,
 In this your concord find:
 May Jesus Christ be praised!
 Let all the earth around
 Ring joyous with the sound:
 May Jesus Christ be praised!

5. In heav'n's eternal bliss,
 The loveliest strain is this:
 May Jesus Christ be praised!
 Let earth, and sea, and sky
 From depth to height reply:
 May Jesus Christ be praised!

6. Be this, while life is mine,
 My canticle divine:
 May Jesus Christ be praised!
 Be this th'eternal song
 Through all the ages long:
 May Jesus Christ be praised!

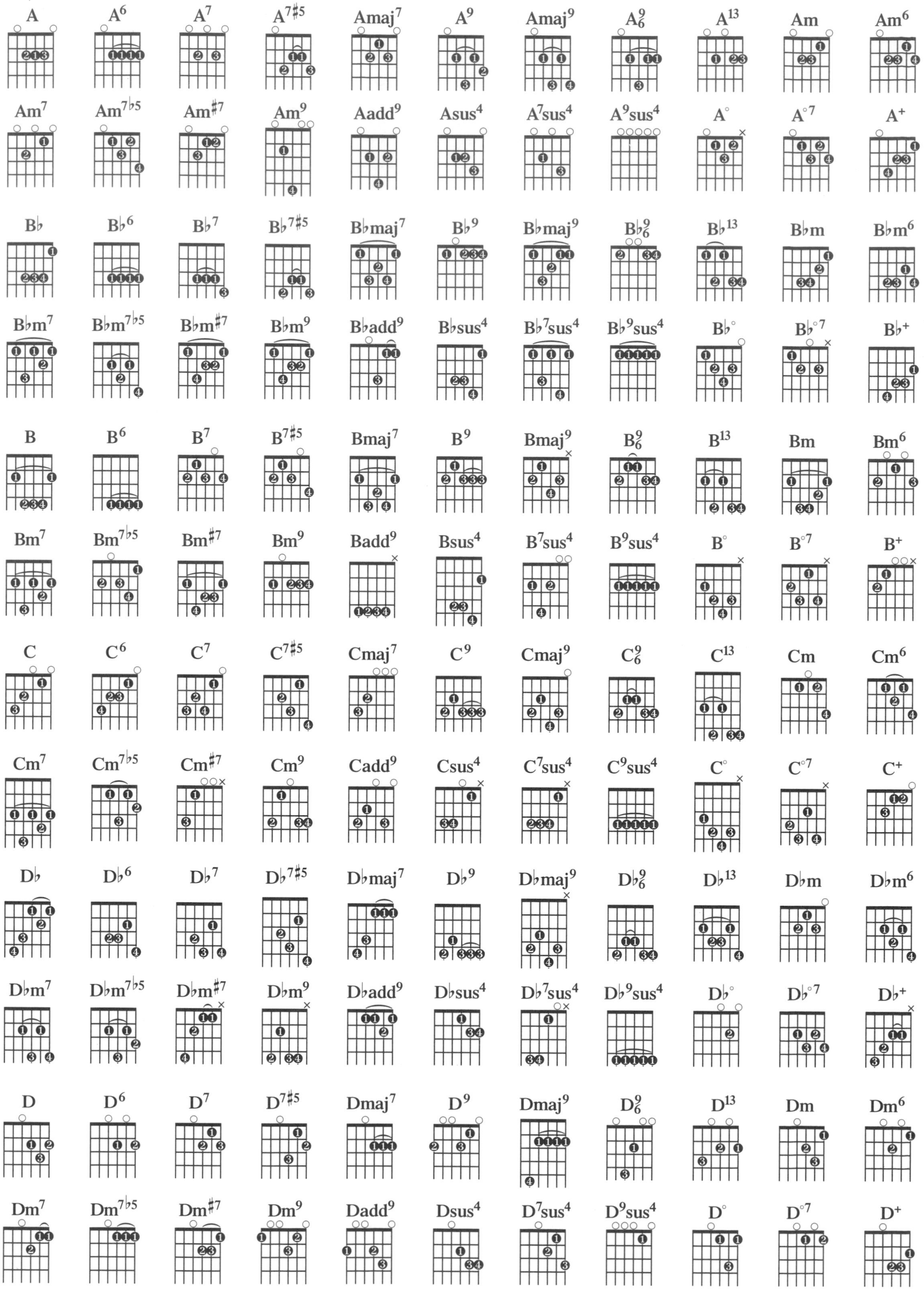
A
A6
A7
A7♯5
Amaj7
A9
Amaj9
A6/9
A13
Am
Am6
Am7
Am7♭5
Am♯7
Am9
Aadd9
Asus4
A7sus4
A9sus4
A°
A°7
A+
B♭
B♭6
B♭7
B♭7♯5
B♭maj7
B♭9
B♭maj9
B♭6/9
B♭13
B♭m
B♭m6
B♭m7
B♭m7♭5
B♭m♯7
B♭m9
B♭add9
B♭sus4
B♭7sus4
B♭9sus4
B♭°
B♭°7
B♭+
B
B6
B7
B7♯5
Bmaj7
B9
Bmaj9
B6/9
B13
Bm
Bm6
Bm7
Bm7♭5
Bm♯7
Bm9
Badd9
Bsus4
B7sus4
B9sus4
B°
B°7
B+
C
C6
C7
C7♯5
Cmaj7
C9
Cmaj9
C6/9
C13
Cm
Cm6
Cm7
Cm7♭5
Cm♯7
Cm9
Cadd9
Csus4
C7sus4
C9sus4
C°
C°7
C+
D♭
D♭6
D♭7
D♭7♯5
D♭maj7
D♭9
D♭maj9
D♭6/9
D♭13
D♭m
D♭m6
D♭m7
D♭m7♭5
D♭m♯7
D♭m9
D♭add9
D♭sus4
D♭7sus4
D♭9sus4
D♭°
D♭°7
D♭+
D
D6
D7
D7♯5
Dmaj7
D9
Dmaj9
D6/9
D13
Dm
Dm6
Dm7
Dm7♭5
Dm♯7
Dm9
Dadd9
Dsus4
D7sus4
D9sus4
D°
D°7
D+